What's Cooking

pasta

What's Cooking

pasta

A collection of must-have recipes for all occasions

First published in 2010

LOVE FOOD is an imprint of Parragon Books Ltd

Parragon

Queen Street House

4 Queen Street

Bath BA1 1HE, UK

ISBN: 978-1-4454-0318-2

Printed in China

Cover design by Talking Design

Cover image by Clive Streeter

Internal design by Simon Levy

Additional photography by Don Last

Food styling by Christine France

Introduction by Linda Doeser

Notes for the reader

This book uses both metric and imperial measurements. Follow the same units of measurement throughout; do not mix metric and imperial. All spoon measurements are level: teaspoons are assumed to be 5 ml, and tablespoons are assumed to be 15 ml. Unless otherwise stated, milk is assumed to be full fat, eggs and individual vegetables are medium, and pepper is freshly ground black pepper.

The times given are an approximate guide only. Preparation times differ according to the techniques used by different people and the cooking times may also vary from those given. Optional ingredients, variations or serving suggestions have not been included in the calculations.

Recipes using raw or very lightly cooked eggs should be avoided by infants, the elderly, pregnant women, convalescents and anyone suffering from an illness. Pregnant and breastfeeding women are advised to avoid eating peanuts and peanut products. Sufferers from nut allergies should be aware that some of the ready-made ingredients used in the recipes in this book may contain nuts. Always check the packaging before use.

Vegetarians should be aware that some of the ready-made ingredients used in the recipes in this book may contain animal products. Always check the packaging before use.

CONTENTS

INTRODUCTION

Pasta is arguably the most useful ingredient to be found in any kitchen. It goes with just about anything else you can think of – from vegetables and cheese to meat and fish. It's equally delicious served with simple, inexpensive sauces or extravagant and luxurious mixtures, and it can be added to soups or form the basis of filling baked dishes. It may be a main meal, a starter or a delightfully different salad.

Pasta is very versatile so it's easy to find fabulous recipes for all occasions and every season of the year. Virtually everyone loves pasta and it's especially popular with children. High in complex carbohydrates, it provides a steady release of energy but contains hardly any fat. Depending on the type of wheat flour used in its manufacture, it can also be a good source of protein, as well as B vitamins, potassium and iron. Moreover, it's economical, convenient and the dried variety keeps well. Huge numbers of pasta dishes can be prepared and cooked within 30 minutes and many take only half that time.

TYPES OF PASTA

There are hundreds of pasta shapes and new ones are being introduced all the time. There are no hard and fast rules about which shape goes with a particular sauce, although there are some traditional partnerships, such as Spaghetti Bolognese. However, there are some useful guidelines.

Long, thin pasta, such as spaghetti and linguine, is ideal for seafood sauces and light olive oil or fresh tomato dressings, but cannot really hold thick or chunky sauces. These are better served with pasta shapes that trap the sauce in hollows and ridges – penne (quills), fusilli (spirals) or conchiglie (shells), for example. Flat ribbons, such as tagliatelle, fettuccine and pappardelle, are perfect for rich or creamy sauces.

Baked dishes are often made with lasagne (flat sheets of pasta that can be layered with a variety of sauces) or cannelloni (tubes that can be filled and baked in a sauce). Smaller shapes, such as macaroni and rigatoni, are also often used in baking.

Very small pasta shapes, such as stellete (stars) and anellini (rings), are used in soups, and filled pasta, such as ravioli and tortellini, is also often served in broth.

BASIC RECIPES

Béchamel Sauce

Makes 300 ml/10 fl oz

Ingredients
300 ml/10 fl oz milk
1 bay leaf
6 black peppercorns
slice of onion
mace blade
25 g/1 oz butter
25 g/1 oz plain flour
salt and pepper

1 Pour the milk into a saucepan and add the bay leaf, peppercorns, onion and mace. Bring to just below boiling point, then remove the pan from the heat, cover and leave to infuse for 10 minutes. Strain the milk into a jug and discard the flavourings.

2 Melt the butter in another saucepan. Sprinkle in the flour and cook over a low heat, stirring constantly, for 2 minutes. Remove the pan from the heat and gradually stir in the milk.

3 Return the pan to a low heat and bring to the boil, stirring constantly. Cook, stirring constantly, until thickened and smooth. Season to taste with salt and pepper.

Pesto

Serves 4

Ingredients
115 g/4 oz fresh basil leaves
25 g/1 oz pine kernels
1 garlic clove, roughly chopped
55 g/2 oz Parmesan cheese, freshly grated
6–8 tbsp extra virgin olive oil
salt

1 Put the basil, pine kernels and garlic in a mortar. Add a pinch of salt and pound to a paste with a pestle.

2 Transfer the mixture to a bowl and gradually work in the Parmesan cheese with a wooden spoon. Gradually stir in the oil until the sauce is thick and creamy. Cover with clingfilm and store in the refrigerator until required.

MAKING FRESH PASTA

If you want to make filled pasta, such as tortellini, you will need to prepare the dough yourself. The same basic dough can also be used to make lasagne sheets and a variety of shapes, such as tagliatelle, pappardelle and macaroni. You need no special equipment and the process is both easy and satisfying.

Basic pasta dough

Serves 3–4
Preparation time: 15 minutes, plus
30 minutes to rest

Ingredients

200 g/7 oz strong white flour,
  plus extra for dusting
pinch of salt
2 eggs, lightly beaten
1 tbsp olive oil

1 Sift together the flour and salt onto a work surface and make a well in the centre with your fingers. Pour the eggs and oil into the well then, using the fingers of one hand, gradually incorporate the flour into the liquid.

2 Knead the dough on a lightly floured work surface until it is completely smooth. Wrap in clingfilm and leave to rest for 30 minutes before rolling out or feeding through a pasta machine. Resting makes the dough more elastic.

Flavoured pasta

Basic pasta dough may be flavoured and coloured by the addition of other ingredients.

Tomato pasta: Add 2 tablespoons of tomato purée to the well in the flour and use only $1^1/_2$ eggs instead of 2.

Spinach pasta: Blanch 225 g/8 oz spinach in boiling water for 1 minute, then drain and squeeze out as much liquid as possible. Alternatively, use 150 g/$5^1/_2$ oz thawed frozen spinach. This does not need blanching, but as much liquid as possible should be squeezed out. Finely chop the spinach and mix with the flour before making a well and adding the eggs and oil.

Herb pasta: Add 3 tablespoons of finely chopped fresh herbs to the flour before making a well and adding the eggs and oil.

Saffron pasta: Soak a sachet of powdered saffron in 2 tablespoons hot water for 15 minutes. Use $1^1/_2$ eggs and whisk the saffron water into them.

Wholemeal pasta: Use 140 g/5 oz wholemeal flour and 25 g/1 oz strong white flour.

Rolling out pasta dough

When the fresh dough has rested, it may be rolled out by hand or with a pasta machine. Larger quantities of dough should be halved or cut into thirds before rolling out. Keep covered until you are ready to work on them.

To roll out by hand, lightly dust a work surface with plain flour, then roll out the pasta dough with a lightly floured rolling pin, always rolling away from you and turning the dough a quarter turn each time. Keep rolling to make a rectangle 2–3 mm/$^1/_{16}$–$^1/_8$ inch thick. The dough can then be cut into ribbons, stamped out with a biscuit cutter or cut into squares to make ravioli.

A pasta machine makes rolling out the dough easier and quicker and ensures that it is even. There are a number of models available, the most useful being a hand-cranked machine with attachable cutters. An electric machine is even easier to use but somewhat extravagant. Cut the dough into manageable sized pieces – 1 quantity Basic Pasta Dough should be cut into 4 pieces, for example. Flatten a piece with your hand and wrap the others in clingfilm until required. Fold the flat piece into thirds and feed it through the pasta machine on its widest setting. Repeat the folding and rolling 3 or 4 more times on this setting, then close the rollers by one notch. Continue feeding the dough through the rollers, without folding into thirds, gradually reducing the setting until you reach the narrowest. If you want to make ribbons, cut the dough into 30-cm/12-inch strips and feed through the appropriate cutter.

SOUPS & SALADS

MINESTRONE MILANESE

Heat the oil in a large heavy-based saucepan. Add the pancetta, onions and garlic and cook, stirring occasionally, for 5 minutes. Add the carrots and celery and cook, stirring occasionally, for a further 5 minutes, or until all the vegetables are softened.

Drain the haricot beans and add them to the saucepan with the tomatoes and their can juices and the beef stock. Bring to the boil, reduce the heat, cover and simmer for 1 hour.

Add the potatoes, re-cover and cook for 15 minutes, then add the pasta, green beans, peas, cabbage and parsley. Cover and cook for a further 15 minutes, until all the vegetables are tender. Season to taste with salt and pepper. Ladle into warmed soup bowls and serve immediately with Parmesan cheese shavings.

SERVES 6

2 tbsp olive oil

55 g/2 oz pancetta, diced

2 onions, sliced

2 garlic cloves, finely chopped

3 carrots, chopped

2 celery sticks, chopped

225 g/8 oz haricot beans, soaked for 3–4 hours

400 g/14 oz canned chopped tomatoes

2 litres/3½ pints beef stock

350 g/12 oz potatoes, diced

175 g/6 oz dried macaroni

175 g/6 oz green beans, sliced

115 g/4 oz fresh or frozen peas

225 g/8 oz Savoy cabbage, shredded

3 tbsp chopped fresh flat-leaf parsley

salt and pepper

fresh Parmesan cheese shavings, to serve

TUSCAN BEAN SOUP

Place half the cannellini beans and half the borlotti beans in a food processor with half the stock and process until smooth. Pour into a large heavy-based saucepan and add the remaining beans. Stir in enough of the remaining stock to achieve the consistency you like, then bring to the boil.

Add the pasta and return to the boil, then reduce the heat and cook for 15 minutes, or until just tender.

Meanwhile, heat 3 tablespoons of the oil in a small frying pan. Add the garlic and cook, stirring constantly, for 2–3 minutes, or until golden. Stir the garlic into the soup with the parsley.

Season to taste with salt and pepper and ladle into warmed soup bowls. Drizzle with the remaining oil to taste and serve immediately.

SERVES 6

300 g/10½ oz canned cannellini beans, drained and rinsed

300 g/10½ oz canned borlotti beans, drained and rinsed

about 600 ml/1 pint chicken or vegetable stock

115 g/4 oz dried conchigliette

4–5 tbsp olive oil

2 garlic cloves, very finely chopped

3 tbsp chopped fresh flat-leaf parsley

salt and pepper

BEAN & PASTA SOUP

Put the beans into a large pan, cover with cold water and bring to the boil. Boil rapidly for 10 minutes to remove any toxins. Drain and rinse.

Heat the oil in a large pan over a medium heat. Add the onions and cook until they are just starting to change colour. Stir in the garlic and cook for a further minute. Stir in the chopped tomatoes, oregano and the tomato purée. Pour over the water.

Add the cooked, drained beans to the mixture in the pan, bring to the boil and cover. Simmer for about 45 minutes, or until the beans are almost tender.

Add the pasta, season to taste with salt and pepper and stir in the sun-dried tomatoes. Return the soup to the boil, partially cover and continue cooking for 10 minutes, or until the pasta is nearly tender.

Stir in the chopped coriander. Taste the soup and adjust the seasoning, if necessary. Ladle the soup into warmed soup bowls, sprinkle with the Parmesan cheese and serve immediately.

SERVES 4

- 225 g/8 oz dried haricot beans, soaked, drained and rinsed
- 4 tbsp olive oil
- 2 large onions, sliced
- 3 garlic cloves, chopped
- 400 g/14 oz canned chopped tomatoes
- 1 tsp dried oregano
- 1 tsp tomato purée
- 850 ml/1½ pints water
- 85 g/3 oz dried macaroni
- 125 g/4½ oz sun-dried tomatoes, drained and thinly sliced
- 1 tbsp chopped fresh coriander or flat-leaf parsley
- 2 tbsp freshly grated Parmesan cheese
- salt and pepper

POTATO & PESTO SOUP

Heat the oil in a large saucepan and cook the bacon over a medium heat for 4 minutes. Add the butter, potatoes and onions and cook for 12 minutes, stirring constantly.

Add the stock and milk to the saucepan, bring to the boil and simmer for 5 minutes. Add the conchigliette and simmer for a further 3–4 minutes.

Blend in the cream and simmer for 5 minutes. Add the parsley, salt and pepper to taste and pesto. Transfer the soup to individual serving bowls and serve with Parmesan cheese.

SERVES 4

2 tbsp olive oil

3 rashers rindless, smoked bacon, finely chopped

25 g/1 oz butter

450 g/1 lb floury potatoes, chopped

450 g/1 lb onions, finely chopped

600 ml/1 pint chicken stock

600 ml/1 pint milk

100 g/3½ oz dried conchigliette

150 ml/5 fl oz double cream

2 tbsp chopped parsley

2 tbsp Pesto (see page 7)

salt and pepper

freshly grated Parmesan cheese, to serve

FRESH TOMATO SOUP

Heat the oil in a large heavy-based saucepan and add the tomatoes, onion, garlic and celery. Cover and cook over a low heat for 45 minutes, occasionally shaking the saucepan gently, until the mixture is pulpy.

Transfer the mixture to a food processor or blender and process to a smooth purée. Push the purée through a sieve into the rinsed-out saucepan.

Add the stock and bring to the boil. Add the pasta, bring back to the boil and cook for 8–10 minutes, until the pasta is tender but still firm to the bite. Season to taste with salt and pepper. Ladle into warmed bowls, sprinkle with the parsley and serve immediately.

SERVES 4

1 tbsp olive oil

650 g/1 lb 7 oz plum tomatoes

1 onion, cut into quarters

1 garlic clove, thinly sliced

1 celery stick, roughly chopped

500 ml/18 fl oz chicken stock

55 g/2 oz dried macaroni

salt and pepper

chopped fresh flat-leaf parsley,
  to garnish

ITALIAN
CHICKEN SOUP

Place the chicken in a large saucepan and pour in the chicken stock and cream. Bring to the boil, then reduce the heat and simmer for 20 minutes.

Meanwhile, bring a large heavy-based saucepan of lightly salted water to the boil. Add the pasta, return to the boil and cook for 8–10 minutes, or until just tender but still firm to the bite. Drain the pasta well and keep warm.

Season the soup with salt and pepper to taste. Mix the cornflour and milk together until a smooth paste forms, then stir it into the soup. Add the sweetcorn and pasta and heat through. Ladle the soup into warmed soup bowls and serve.

SERVES 4

450 g/1 lb skinless, boneless chicken breasts, cut into thin strips

1.2 litres/2 pints chicken stock

150 ml/5 fl oz double cream

115 g/4 oz dried vermicelli

1 tbsp cornflour

3 tbsp milk

175 g/6 oz canned sweetcorn kernels, drained

salt and pepper

CHICKEN & PASTA BROTH

Put the chicken into a large flameproof casserole dish with the water, celery, carrot, onion, leek, garlic, peppercorns, allspice, herbs and ½ teaspoon of salt. Bring just to the boil over a medium heat and skim off the scum that rises to the surface. Reduce the heat, partially cover and simmer for 2 hours.

Remove the chicken from the stock and leave to cool. Continue simmering the stock, uncovered, for about 30 minutes. When the chicken is cool enough to handle, remove the meat from the bones and, if necessary, cut into bite-sized pieces.

Strain the stock and remove as much fat as possible. Discard the vegetables and flavourings. (There should be about 1.7 litres/3 pints chicken stock.)

Bring the stock to the boil in a clean pan over a medium heat. Add the pasta and reduce the heat so the stock simmers very gently. Cook for 8–10 minutes, or until the pasta is tender but still firm to the bite.

Stir in the chicken. Taste and adjust the seasoning. Ladle into bowls, sprinkle with parsley and serve.

SERVES 4–6

1.25 kg/2 lb 12 oz chicken pieces, such as wings or legs

2.5 litres/4½ pints water

1 celery stick, sliced

1 large carrot, sliced

1 onion, sliced

1 leek, sliced

2 garlic cloves, finely chopped

8 peppercorns

4 allspice berries

3–4 fresh parsley stems

2–3 fresh thyme sprigs

1 bay leaf

85 g/3 oz dried farfalline

salt and pepper

chopped fresh parsley, to garnish

FISH SOUP WITH MACARONI

Heat the oil in a large heavy-based saucepan. Add the onions and garlic and cook over a low heat, stirring occasionally, for 5 minutes, or until the onions have softened.

Add the stock with the tomatoes and their can juices, herbs, saffron and pasta and season to taste with salt and pepper. Bring to the boil, then cover and simmer for 15 minutes.

Discard any mussels with broken shells or any that refuse to close when tapped. Add the mussels, monkfish and prawns to the saucepan. Re-cover the saucepan and simmer for a further 5–10 minutes, until the mussels have opened, the prawns have changed colour and the fish is opaque and flakes easily. Discard any mussels that remain closed. Ladle the soup into warmed bowls and serve.

SERVES 6

2 tbsp olive oil

2 onions, sliced

1 garlic clove, finely chopped

1 litre/1¾ pints fish stock or water

400 g/14 oz canned chopped tomatoes

¼ tsp herbes de Provence

¼ tsp saffron threads

115 g/4 oz dried macaroni

18 live mussels, scrubbed and debearded

450 g/1 lb monkfish fillet, cut into chunks

225 g/8 oz raw prawns, peeled and deveined, tails left on

salt and pepper

MUSSEL & PASTA SOUP

Discard any mussels with broken shells or any that refuse to close when tapped. Bring a large heavy-based saucepan of water to the boil. Add the mussels and oil and season to taste with pepper. Cover tightly and cook over a high heat for 5 minutes, or until the mussels have opened. Remove the mussels with a slotted spoon, discarding any that remain closed. Strain the cooking liquid through a muslin-lined sieve and reserve 1.2 litres/2 pints.

Melt the butter in a clean saucepan. Add the bacon, onion and garlic and cook over a low heat, stirring occasionally, for 5 minutes. Stir in the flour and cook, stirring, for 1 minute. Gradually stir in all but 2 tablespoons of the reserved cooking liquid and bring to the boil, stirring constantly. Add the potato slices and simmer for 5 minutes. Add the pasta and simmer for a further 10 minutes.

Stir in the cream and lemon juice and season to taste with salt and pepper. Add the mussels. Mix the egg yolks and the remaining mussel cooking liquid together, then stir the mixture into the soup and cook for 4 minutes, until thickened.

Ladle the soup into warmed soup bowls, garnish with chopped parsley and serve immediately.

SERVES 4

750 g/1 lb 10 oz mussels, scrubbed and debearded

2 tbsp olive oil

100 g/3½ oz butter

55 g/2 oz rindless streaky bacon, chopped

1 onion, chopped

2 garlic cloves, finely chopped

55 g/2 oz plain flour

3 potatoes, thinly sliced

115 g/4 oz dried farfalle

300 ml/10 fl oz double cream

1 tbsp lemon juice

2 egg yolks

salt and pepper

2 tbsp finely chopped fresh parsley, to garnish

PASTA SALAD
WITH WALNUTS
& DOLCELATTE

Bring a large heavy-based saucepan of lightly salted water to the boil. Add the pasta, return to the boil and cook for 8–10 minutes, or until tender but still firm to the bite. Drain and refresh in a bowl of cold water. Drain again.

Mix the walnut oil, safflower oil and vinegar together in a jug, whisking well, and season to taste with salt and pepper.

Arrange the salad leaves in a large serving bowl. Top with the pasta, dolcelatte cheese and walnuts. Pour the dressing over the salad, toss lightly and serve.

SERVES 4

225 g/8 oz dried farfalle

2 tbsp walnut oil

4 tbsp safflower oil

2 tbsp balsamic vinegar

280 g/10 oz mixed salad leaves

225 g/8 oz dolcelatte cheese, diced

115 g/4 oz walnuts halves, toasted

salt and pepper

PASTA SALAD WITH PESTO VINAIGRETTE

Bring a large pan of lightly salted water to the boil over a medium heat. Add the pasta and cook for about 8–10 minutes, or until tender but still firm to the bite. Drain, rinse in hot water, then drain again and reserve.

To make the pesto vinaigrette, whisk the basil, garlic, Parmesan cheese, oil and lemon juice together in a small bowl until well blended. Season to taste with pepper.

Put the pasta into a bowl, pour over the pesto vinaigrette and toss thoroughly.

Cut the tomatoes into wedges. Halve and stone the olives and slice the sun-dried tomatoes. Add the tomatoes, olives and sun-dried tomatoes to the pasta and toss well.

Transfer the pasta mixture to a salad bowl and scatter the pine kernels and Parmesan cheese over the top. Garnish with a fresh basil sprig and serve warm.

SERVES 6

225 g/8 oz dried fusilli

4 tomatoes, peeled

55 g/2 oz black olives

25 g/1 oz sun-dried tomatoes in oil, drained

2 tbsp pine kernels, toasted

2 tbsp freshly grated Parmesan cheese

salt

1 fresh basil sprig, to garnish

pesto vinaigrette

4 tbsp chopped fresh basil

1 garlic clove, very finely chopped

2 tbsp freshly grated Parmesan cheese

4 tbsp olive oil

2 tbsp lemon juice

pepper

PASTA SALAD
WITH
CHARGRILLED
PEPPERS

Put the whole peppers on a baking sheet and place under a preheated grill, turning frequently, for 15 minutes, until charred all over. Remove with tongs and place in a bowl. Cover with crumpled kitchen paper and set aside.

Meanwhile, bring a large saucepan of lightly salted water to the boil. Add the pasta, bring back to the boil and cook for 8–10 minutes, until tender but still firm to the bite.

Combine the oil, lemon juice, pesto and garlic in a bowl, whisking well to mix. Drain the pasta, add it to the pesto mixture while still hot and toss well. Set aside.

When the peppers are cool enough to handle, peel off the skins, then cut open and remove the seeds. Chop the flesh roughly and add to the pasta with the basil. Season to taste with salt and pepper and toss well. Serve at room temperature.

SERVES 4

1 red pepper

1 orange pepper

280 g/10 oz dried conchiglie

5 tbsp extra virgin olive oil

2 tbsp lemon juice

2 tbsp Pesto (see page 7)

1 garlic clove, crushed

3 tbsp shredded fresh basil leaves

salt and pepper

PASTA & CHICKEN MEDLEY

To make the dressing, whisk the vinegar and oil together well, then season to taste with salt and pepper.

Bring a large saucepan of lightly salted water to the boil. Add the pasta, bring back to the boil and cook for 8–10 minutes, until tender but still firm to the bite. Drain thoroughly, rinse and drain again. Transfer to a bowl and mix in 1 tablespoon of the dressing while hot, then set aside until cold.

Combine the mayonnaise, pesto and soured cream in a bowl, and season to taste with salt and pepper.

Add the chicken, celery, grapes, carrot and the mayonnaise mixture to the pasta, and toss thoroughly. Check the seasoning, adding more salt and pepper if necessary.

Arrange the pasta mixture in a large serving bowl, garnish with the celery leaves and serve.

SERVES 2

125–150 g/4½–5½ oz dried fusilli

2 tbsp mayonnaise

2 tsp Pesto (see page 7)

1 tbsp soured cream or natural fromage frais

175 g/6 oz cooked skinless, boneless chicken, cut into strips

1–2 celery sticks, sliced diagonally

125 g/4½ oz black grapes, halved and deseeded

1 large carrot, cut into strips

salt and pepper

celery leaves, to garnish

dressing

1 tbsp white wine vinegar

3 tbsp extra virgin olive oil

salt and pepper

RARE BEEF
PASTA SALAD

Season the steak to taste with salt and pepper, then grill or pan-fry for 4 minutes on each side. Leave to rest for 5 minutes, then, using a sharp knife, slice the steak thinly across the grain and reserve until required.

Meanwhile, bring a large pan of lightly salted water to the boil over a medium heat. Add the pasta and cook for 8–10 minutes, until tender but still firm to the bite. Drain thoroughly, refresh in cold water and drain again. Toss the pasta in the oil.

Mix the lime juice, fish sauce and honey together in a small pan and cook over a medium heat for about 2 minutes.

Add the spring onions, cucumber, tomato wedges and mint to the pan, then add the steak and mix well. Season with salt to taste.

Transfer the pasta to a large warmed serving dish and top with the steak mixture. Serve just warm or leave to cool completely.

SERVES 4

450 g/1 lb rump or sirloin
   steak in 1 piece

450 g/1 lb dried fusilli

4 tbsp olive oil

2 tbsp lime juice

2 tbsp Thai fish sauce

2 tsp clear honey

4 spring onions, sliced

1 cucumber, peeled and cut into
   2.5-cm/1-inch chunks

3 tomatoes, cut into wedges

3 tsp finely chopped fresh mint

salt and pepper

SPICY SAUSAGE SALAD

Bring a pan of lightly salted water to the boil over a medium heat. Add the pasta and cook for 8–10 minutes, or until tender but still firm to the bite. Drain thoroughly and reserve.

Heat the oil in a pan over a medium heat. Add the onion and cook until translucent. Stir in the garlic, yellow pepper and sausage and cook for about 3–4 minutes, stirring once or twice.

Add the wine, vinegar and reserved pasta to the pan, stir and bring the mixture just to the boil over a medium heat.

Arrange the salad leaves on large serving plates, spoon over the warm sausage and pasta mixture and serve immediately.

SERVES 4

125 g/4½ oz dried conchiglie

2 tbsp olive oil

1 medium onion, chopped

2 garlic cloves, very finely chopped

1 small yellow pepper, deseeded and cut into matchsticks

175 g/6 oz spicy pork sausage, such as chorizo, Italian pepperoni or salami, skinned and sliced

2 tbsp red wine

1 tbsp red wine vinegar

125 g/4½ oz mixed salad leaves

salt

NIÇOISE PASTA SALAD

Bring a large pan of lightly salted water to the boil over a medium heat. Add the pasta and cook for 8–10 minutes, until tender but still firm to the bite. Drain and refresh in cold water.

Bring a small pan of lightly salted water to the boil over a medium heat. Add the green beans and cook for 10–12 minutes, or until tender but still firm to the bite. Drain, refresh in cold water, drain again and reserve.

Put the anchovies in a shallow bowl, pour over the milk and leave to stand for 10 minutes. Meanwhile, tear the lettuces into large pieces. Blanch the tomatoes in boiling water for 1–2 minutes, then drain, skin and roughly chop the flesh. Shell the eggs and cut into quarters. Flake the tuna into large chunks.

Drain the anchovies and the pasta. Put all the salad ingredients into a large bowl and gently mix together.

To make the vinaigrette dressing, beat together the oil, vinegar and mustard and season to taste with salt and pepper. Chill in the refrigerator until required. Just before serving, pour the vinaigrette dressing over the salad.

SERVES 4

350 g/12 oz dried conchiglie

115 g/4 oz green beans

50 g/1¾ oz canned anchovy fillets, drained

2 tbsp milk

2 small crisp lettuces

3 large beef tomatoes

4 hard-boiled eggs

225 g/8 oz canned tuna, drained

115 g/4 oz stoned black olives

salt

vinaigrette dressing

3 tbsp extra virgin olive oil

2 tbsp white wine vinegar

1 tsp wholegrain mustard

salt and pepper

PASTA SALAD
WITH MELON &
PRAWNS

Bring a large pan of salted water to the boil. Add the pasta,
bring back to the boil and cook for 8–10 minutes, until tender
but still firm to the bite. Drain, toss with 1 tablespoon of the oil
and leave to cool.

Meanwhile, peel and devein the prawns, then place them in a
large bowl. Halve both the melons and scoop out the seeds with
a spoon. Using a melon baller or teaspoon, scoop out balls of the
flesh and add them to the prawns.

Whisk together the remaining oil, the vinegar, mustard, sugar,
parsley and chopped basil in a small bowl. Season to taste
with salt and pepper. Add the cooled pasta to the prawn and
melon mixture and toss lightly to mix, then pour in the dressing
and toss again. Cover with clingfilm and chill in the refrigerator
for 30 minutes.

Make a bed of shredded lettuce on a serving plate. Spoon the
pasta salad on top, garnish with basil sprigs and serve.

SERVES 6

225 g/8 oz dried green fusilli

5 tbsp extra virgin olive oil

450 g/1 lb cooked prawns

1 Charentais melon

1 Galia melon

1 tbsp red wine vinegar

1 tsp Dijon mustard

pinch of caster sugar

1 tbsp chopped fresh flat-leaf
parsley

1 tbsp chopped fresh basil,
plus extra sprigs to garnish

1 oakleaf or quattro stagioni
lettuce, shredded

salt and pepper

MEAT & POULTRY

SPAGHETTI BOLOGNESE

Heat the oil in a large frying pan. Add the onion and cook for 3 minutes. Add the garlic, carrot, celery and pancetta and sauté for 3–4 minutes, or until just beginning to brown.

Add the beef and cook over a high heat for another 3 minutes or until all of the meat is browned. Stir in the tomatoes, oregano and wine and bring to the boil. Reduce the heat and leave to simmer for about 45 minutes.

Stir in the tomato purée and season to taste with salt and pepper.

Bring a large saucepan of lightly salted water to the boil. Add the pasta, bring back to the boil and cook for 8–10 minutes, until tender but still firm to the bite. Drain thoroughly.

Transfer the spaghetti to a serving plate and pour over the bolognese sauce. Toss to mix well, garnish with parsley and serve hot.

SERVES 4

1 tbsp olive oil

1 onion, finely chopped

2 garlic cloves, chopped

1 carrot, chopped

1 celery stick, chopped

50 g/1¾ oz pancetta or streaky bacon, diced

350 g/12 oz fresh lean beef mince

400 g/14 oz canned chopped tomatoes

2 tsp dried oregano

125 ml/4 fl oz red wine

2 tbsp tomato purée

350 g/12 oz dried spaghetti

salt and pepper

chopped fresh parsley, to garnish

SPAGHETTI WITH MEATBALLS

Place the potato in a small pan, add cold water to cover and a pinch of salt and bring to the boil. Cook for 10–15 minutes, until tender, then drain. Either mash thoroughly with a potato masher or fork, or pass through a potato ricer.

Combine the potato, beef, onion, egg and parsley in a bowl and season to taste with salt and pepper. Spread out the flour on a plate. With dampened hands, shape the meat mixture into walnut-sized balls and roll in the flour. Shake off any excess.

Heat the oil in a heavy-based frying pan, add the meatballs and cook over a medium heat, stirring and turning frequently, for 8–10 minutes, until golden all over.

Add the passata and tomato purée and cook for a further 10 minutes, until the sauce is reduced and thickened.

Meanwhile, bring a large saucepan of lightly salted water to the boil. Add the pasta, bring back to the boil and cook for 8–10 minutes, or until tender but still firm to the bite.

Drain well and add to the meatball sauce, tossing well to coat. Transfer to a warmed serving dish, garnish with the basil and serve immediately with freshly grated Parmesan cheese.

SERVES 6

1 potato, diced

400 g/14 oz fresh beef mince

1 onion, finely chopped

1 egg

4 tbsp chopped fresh flat-leaf parsley

plain flour, for dusting

5 tbsp olive oil

400 ml/14 fl oz passata

2 tbsp tomato purée

400 g/14 oz dried spaghetti

salt and pepper

shredded fresh basil, to garnish

freshly grated Parmesan cheese, to serve

SPAGHETTI ALLA CARBONARA

Bring a large heavy-based saucepan of lightly salted water to the boil. Add the pasta, return to the boil and cook for 8–10 minutes, or until tender but still firm to the bite.

Meanwhile, heat the oil in a heavy-based frying pan. Add the pancetta and cook over a medium heat, stirring frequently, for 8–10 minutes.

Beat the eggs with the cream in a small bowl and season to taste with salt and pepper. Drain the pasta and return it to the saucepan. Tip in the contents of the frying pan, then add the egg mixture and half the Parmesan cheese. Stir well, then transfer to a warmed serving dish. Serve immediately, sprinkled with the remaining cheese.

SERVES 4

450 g/1 lb dried spaghetti

1 tbsp olive oil

225 g/8 oz rindless pancetta or streaky bacon, chopped

4 eggs

5 tbsp single cream

2 tbsp freshly grated Parmesan cheese

salt and pepper

LINGUINE WITH BACON & OLIVES

Heat the oil in a large frying pan. Add the onions, garlic and bacon and cook over a low heat, stirring occasionally, until the onions are softened. Stir in the mushrooms, anchovies and olives, then season to taste with salt, if necessary, and pepper. Simmer for 5 minutes.

Meanwhile, bring a large heavy-based saucepan of lightly salted water to the boil. Add the pasta, return to the boil and cook for 8–10 minutes, or until tender but still firm to the bite.

Drain the pasta and transfer to a warmed serving dish. Spoon the sauce on top, toss lightly and sprinkle with the Parmesan cheese. Serve immediately.

SERVES 4

3 tbsp olive oil

2 onions, thinly sliced

2 garlic cloves, finely chopped

175 g/6 oz rindless lean bacon, diced

225 g/8 oz mushrooms, sliced

5 canned anchovy fillets, drained

6 black olives, stoned and halved

450 g/1 lb dried linguine

25 g/1 oz freshly grated Parmesan cheese

salt and pepper

PENNE WITH HAM, TOMATO & CHILLI SAUCE

Put the oil and 1 tablespoon of the butter in a large saucepan over a medium–low heat. Add the onion and cook for 10 minutes, or until soft and golden. Add the ham and cook for 5 minutes, or until lightly browned. Stir in the garlic, chilli and tomatoes. Season to taste with salt and pepper. Bring to the boil, then simmer over a medium–low heat for 30–40 minutes, until thickened.

Meanwhile, bring a large heavy-based saucepan of lightly salted water to the boil. Add the pasta, return to the boil and cook for 8–10 minutes, or until tender but still firm to the bite. Drain and transfer to a warmed serving dish.

Pour the sauce over the pasta. Add the parsley, Parmesan cheese and the remaining butter. Toss well to mix and serve immediately.

SERVES 4

1 tbsp olive oil

2 tbsp butter

1 onion, finely chopped

150 g/5½ oz ham, diced

2 garlic cloves, very finely chopped

1 fresh red chilli, deseeded and finely chopped

800 g/1 lb 12 oz canned chopped tomatoes

450 g/1 lb dried penne

2 tbsp chopped fresh flat-leaf parsley

6 tbsp freshly grated Parmesan cheese

salt and pepper

FARFALLE WITH GORGONZOLA & HAM

Pour the crème fraîche into a saucepan, add the mushrooms and season to taste with salt and pepper. Bring to just below the boil, then lower the heat and simmer very gently, stirring occasionally, for 8–10 minutes, until thickened.

Meanwhile, bring a large pan of lightly salted water to the boil. Add the pasta, bring back to the boil and cook for 8–10 minutes, until tender but still firm to the bite.

Remove the pan containing the mushroom mixture from the heat and stir in the Gorgonzola cheese until it has melted. Return the pan to a very low heat and stir in the chopped parsley and ham.

Drain the pasta and add it to the sauce. Toss lightly, then divide between individual warmed plates, garnish with parsley sprigs and serve.

SERVES 4

225 ml/8 fl oz crème fraîche

225 g/8 oz chestnut mushrooms, quartered

400 g/14 oz dried farfalle

85 g/3 oz Gorgonzola cheese, crumbled

1 tbsp chopped fresh flat-leaf parsley, plus extra sprigs to garnish

175 g/6 oz cooked ham, diced

salt and pepper

PEPPERONI
PASTA

Heat 2 tablespoons of the oil in a large heavy-based frying pan. Add the onion and cook over a low heat, stirring occasionally, for 5 minutes, or until softened. Add the red and orange peppers, tomatoes and their can juices, sun-dried tomato paste and paprika and bring to the boil.

Add the pepperoni and parsley and season to taste with salt and pepper. Stir well, bring to the boil, then reduce the heat and simmer for 10–15 minutes.

Meanwhile, bring a large heavy-based saucepan of lightly salted water to the boil. Add the pasta, return to the boil and cook for 8–10 minutes, or until tender but still firm to the bite. Drain well and transfer to a warmed serving dish. Add the remaining olive oil and toss. Add the sauce and toss again. Sprinkle with parsley and serve immediately.

SERVES 4

3 tbsp olive oil

1 onion, chopped

1 red pepper, deseeded and diced

1 orange pepper, deseeded and diced

800 g/1 lb 12 oz canned chopped tomatoes

1 tbsp sun-dried tomato paste

1 tsp paprika

225 g/8 oz pepperoni sausage, sliced

2 tbsp chopped fresh flat-leaf parsley, plus extra to garnish

450 g/1 lb dried penne

salt and pepper

MACARONI WITH SAUSAGE, PEPPERONCINI & OLIVES

Heat the oil in a large frying pan over a medium heat. Add the onion and cook for 5 minutes, until softened. Add the garlic and cook for a few seconds, until just beginning to colour. Add the sausage and cook until evenly browned.

Stir in the pepperoncini, tomatoes, oregano and stock. Season to taste with salt and pepper. Bring to the boil, then simmer over a medium heat for 10 minutes, stirring occasionally.

Meanwhile, bring a large saucepan of lightly salted water to the boil. Add the pasta, bring back to the boil and cook for 8–10 minutes, or until tender but still firm to the bite. Drain and transfer to a warmed serving dish.

Add the olives and half the cheese to the sauce, then stir until the cheese has melted.

Pour the sauce over the pasta. Toss well to mix. Sprinkle with the remaining cheese and serve immediately.

SERVES 6

1 tbsp olive oil

1 large onion, finely chopped

2 garlic cloves, very finely chopped

450 g/1 lb pork sausage, peeled and roughly chopped

3 canned pepperoncini, or other hot red peppers, drained and sliced

400 g/14 oz canned chopped tomatoes

2 tsp dried oregano

125 ml/4 fl oz chicken stock or red wine

450 g/1 lb dried macaroni

12–15 stoned black olives, quartered

75 g/2¾ oz freshly grated cheese, such as Cheddar or Gruyère

salt and pepper

PASTA & PORK IN CREAM SAUCE

To make the red wine sauce, heat the oil in a small heavy-based saucepan, add the onion and cook until translucent. Stir in the tomato purée, red wine and oregano. Heat gently to reduce and set aside.

Pound the slices of pork between 2 sheets of clingfilm until wafer thin, then cut into strips. Heat the oil in a frying pan, add the pork and cook for 5 minutes. Add the mushrooms and cook for a further 2 minutes. Strain and pour over the red wine sauce. Reduce the heat and simmer for 20 minutes.

Meanwhile, bring a large heavy-based saucepan of lightly salted water to the boil. Add the lemon juice, saffron and pasta, return to the boil and cook for 8–10 minutes, or until tender but still firm to the bite. Drain the pasta thoroughly, return to the saucepan and keep warm.

Stir the cream into the saucepan with the pork and heat for a few minutes.

Boil the quail eggs for 3 minutes, cool them in cold water and remove the shells. Transfer the pasta to a large warmed serving plate, top with the pork and the sauce and garnish with the eggs. Serve immediately.

SERVES 4

450 g/1 lb pork fillet, thinly sliced

4 tbsp olive oil

225 g/8 oz button mushrooms, sliced

1 tbsp lemon juice

pinch of saffron threads

350 g/12 oz dried orecchiette

4 tbsp double cream

12 quail eggs

salt

red wine sauce

1 tbsp olive oil

1 onion, chopped

1 tbsp tomato purée

200 ml/7 fl oz red wine

1 tsp finely chopped fresh oregano

TAGLIATELLE WITH SPRING LAMB

Using a sharp knife, cut small pockets all over the lamb, then insert a garlic slice and a few rosemary leaves in each one. Heat 2 tablespoons of the oil in a large heavy-based frying pan. Add the lamb and cook over a medium heat, turning occasionally, for 25–30 minutes, until tender and cooked to your liking.

Meanwhile, chop the remaining rosemary and place in a mortar. Add the remaining oil and pound with a pestle. Season to taste with salt and pepper and set aside.

Remove the lamb from the heat, cover with foil and leave to stand. Bring a large pan of lightly salted water to the boil. Add the pasta, bring back to the boil and cook for 8–10 minutes, until tender but still firm to the bite.

Meanwhile, melt the butter in another pan. Add the mushrooms and cook over a medium–low heat, stirring occasionally, for 5–8 minutes, until tender.

Drain the pasta, return it to the pan and toss with half the rosemary oil. Uncover the lamb and cut it into slices. Divide the tagliatelle between individual warmed plates, season with pepper and top with the lamb and mushrooms. Drizzle with the remaining rosemary oil, sprinkle with the pecorino cheese and serve immediately.

SERVES 4

750 g/1 lb 10 oz boneless lean lamb in a single piece

6 garlic cloves, thinly sliced

6–8 fresh rosemary sprigs

125 ml/4 fl oz olive oil

400 g/14 oz dried tagliatelle

55 g/2 oz butter

175 g/6 oz button mushrooms

salt and pepper

fresh pecorino cheese shavings, to serve

SPAGHETTI WITH PARSLEY CHICKEN

Heat the oil in a heavy-based saucepan. Add the lemon rind and cook over a low heat, stirring frequently, for 5 minutes. Stir in the ginger and sugar, season to taste with salt and cook, stirring constantly, for a further 2 minutes. Pour in the stock, bring to the boil, then cook for 5 minutes, or until the liquid has reduced by half.

Meanwhile, bring a large heavy-based saucepan of lightly salted water to the boil. Add the pasta, return to the boil and cook for 8–10 minutes, or until tender but still firm to the bite.

Melt half the butter in a frying pan. Add the chicken and onion and cook, stirring frequently, for 5 minutes, or until the chicken is lightly browned all over. Stir in the lemon and ginger mixture and cook for 1 minute. Stir in the parsley leaves and cook, stirring constantly, for a further 3 minutes.

Drain the pasta and transfer to a warmed serving dish, then add the remaining butter and toss well. Add the chicken sauce, toss again and serve.

SERVES 4

1 tbsp olive oil

thinly pared rind of 1 lemon, cut into julienne strips

1 tsp finely chopped fresh ginger

1 tsp sugar

225 ml/8 fl oz chicken stock

250 g/9 oz dried spaghetti

55 g/2 oz butter

225 g/8 oz skinless, boneless chicken breasts, diced

1 red onion, finely chopped

leaves from 2 bunches of flat-leaf parsley

salt

PAPPARDELLE
WITH CHICKEN
& PORCINI

Place the porcini in a small bowl, add the hot water and leave to soak for 20 minutes. Meanwhile, place the tomatoes and their can juices in a heavy-based saucepan and break them up with a wooden spoon, then stir in the chilli. Bring to the boil, reduce the heat and simmer, stirring occasionally, for 30 minutes, or until reduced.

Remove the mushrooms from their soaking liquid with a slotted spoon, reserving the liquid. Strain the liquid through a coffee filter paper or muslin-lined sieve into the tomatoes and simmer for a further 15 minutes.

Meanwhile, heat 2 tablespoons of the oil in a heavy-based frying pan. Add the chicken and cook, stirring frequently, until golden brown all over and tender. Stir in the mushrooms and garlic and cook for a further 5 minutes.

Meanwhile, bring a large heavy-based saucepan of lightly salted water to the boil. Add the pasta, return to the boil and cook for 8–10 minutes, or until tender but still firm to the bite. Drain well, transfer to a warmed serving dish, drizzle with the remaining oil and toss lightly. Stir the chicken mixture into the tomato sauce, season to taste with salt and pepper and spoon on top of the pasta. Toss lightly, sprinkle with parsley and serve immediately.

SERVES 4

40 g/1½ oz dried porcini mushrooms

175 ml/6 fl oz hot water

800 g/1 lb 12 oz canned chopped tomatoes

1 fresh red chilli, deseeded and finely chopped

3 tbsp olive oil

350 g/12 oz skinless, boneless chicken, cut into thin strips

2 garlic cloves, finely chopped

350 g/12 oz dried pappardelle

salt and pepper

2 tbsp chopped fresh flat-leaf parsley, to garnish

PENNE WITH CHICKEN & FETA

Heat the oil in a heavy-based frying pan. Add the chicken and cook over a medium heat, stirring frequently, for 5–8 minutes, or until golden all over and cooked through. Add the spring onions and cook for 2 minutes. Stir the feta cheese into the frying pan with half the chives and season to taste with salt and pepper.

Meanwhile, bring a large heavy-based saucepan of lightly salted water to the boil. Add the pasta, return to the boil and cook for 8–10 minutes, or until tender but still firm to the bite. Drain well, then transfer to a warmed serving dish.

Spoon the chicken mixture onto the pasta, toss lightly and serve immediately, garnished with the remaining chives.

72

SERVES 4

2 tbsp olive oil

450 g/1 lb skinless, boneless chicken breasts, cut into thin strips

6 spring onions, chopped

225 g/8 oz feta cheese, diced

4 tbsp snipped fresh chives

450 g/1 lb dried penne

salt and pepper

FARFALLE WITH CHICKEN & BROCCOLI

Bring a large pan of salted water to the boil. Meanwhile, heat the oil and butter in a large frying pan over a medium–low heat. Cook the garlic until just beginning to colour.

Add the diced chicken, increase the heat to medium and cook for 4–5 minutes, until the chicken is no longer pink. Add the chilli flakes and season to taste with salt and pepper. Remove from the heat.

Plunge the broccoli into the boiling water and cook for 2 minutes. Remove with a slotted spoon and set aside. Bring the water back to the boil. Add the pasta and cook for 8–10 minutes, or until tender but still firm to the bite. Drain and add to the chicken mixture in the frying pan. Add the broccoli and roasted peppers. Pour in the stock. Simmer briskly over a medium–high heat, stirring frequently, until most of the liquid has been absorbed.

Transfer to warmed dishes and serve.

SERVES 4

4 tbsp olive oil

5 tbsp butter

3 garlic cloves, very finely chopped

450 g/1 lb skinless, boneless chicken breasts, diced

$\frac{1}{4}$ tsp dried chilli flakes

450 g/1 lb small broccoli florets

300 g/10$\frac{1}{2}$ oz dried farfalle

175 g/6 oz bottled roasted red peppers, drained and diced

250 ml/9 fl oz chicken stock

salt and pepper

FETTUCCINE
WITH CHICKEN
& BASIL PESTO

To make the pesto, put the basil, olive oil, pine kernels, garlic and a generous pinch of salt in a food processor or blender. Process the ingredients until smooth. Scrape the mixture into a bowl and stir in the cheeses.

Heat the vegetable oil in a frying pan over a medium heat. Cook the chicken breasts, turning once, for 8–10 minutes, until the juices are no longer pink. Cut into small cubes.

Meanwhile, bring a large saucepan of lightly salted water to the boil. Add the pasta, bring back to the boil and cook for 8–10 minutes, or until tender but still firm to the bite. Drain and transfer to a warmed serving dish. Add the chicken and pesto, then season to taste with pepper. Toss well to mix.

Garnish with a sprig of basil and serve warm.

SERVES 4

2 tbsp vegetable oil

4 skinless, boneless chicken breasts

350 g/12 oz dried fettuccine

salt and pepper

sprig of fresh basil, to garnish

pesto

100 g/3½ oz shredded fresh basil

125 ml/4 fl oz extra virgin olive oil

3 tbsp pine kernels

3 garlic cloves, crushed

55 g/2 oz freshly grated Parmesan cheese

2 tbsp freshly grated pecorino cheese

salt

PENNE WITH TURKEY MEATBALLS

Put the turkey, garlic and parsley in a bowl and mix well. Stir in the egg and season to taste with salt and pepper. Dust your hands lightly with flour and shape the mixture into walnut-sized balls between your palms. Lightly dust each meatball with flour.

Heat the oil in a saucepan. Add the onion, celery and carrot and cook over a low heat, stirring occasionally, for 5 minutes, until softened. Increase the heat to medium, add the meatballs and cook, turning frequently, for 8–10 minutes, until golden brown all over.

Pour in the passata, add the rosemary and bay leaf, season to taste with salt and pepper and bring to the boil. Lower the heat, cover and simmer gently, stirring occasionally, for 40–45 minutes. Remove and discard the herbs.

Shortly before the meatballs are ready, bring a large pan of lightly salted water to the boil. Add the pasta, bring back to the boil and cook for 8–10 minutes, until tender but still firm to the bite. Drain and add to the pan with the meatballs. Stir gently and heat through briefly, then spoon into individual warmed dishes. Sprinkle generously with Parmesan cheese and serve immediately.

SERVES 4

350 g/12 oz fresh turkey mince

1 small garlic clove, finely chopped

2 tbsp finely chopped fresh parsley

1 egg, lightly beaten

plain flour, for dusting

3 tbsp olive oil

1 onion, finely chopped

1 celery stick, finely chopped

1 carrot, finely chopped

400 ml/14 fl oz passata

1 fresh rosemary sprig

1 bay leaf

350 g/12 oz dried penne

salt and pepper

freshly grated Parmesan cheese, to serve

FETTUCCINE WITH DUCK SAUCE

Heat half the oil in a frying pan. Add the duck and cook over a medium heat, turning frequently, for 8–10 minutes, until golden brown. Using a slotted spoon, transfer to a large saucepan.

Wipe out the frying pan with kitchen paper, then add the remaining oil. Add the shallot, leek, garlic, celery, carrot and pancetta and cook over a low heat, stirring, for 10 minutes. Using a slotted spoon, transfer the mixture to the pan with the duck and stir in the parsley. Add the bay leaf and season to taste with salt and pepper. Pour in the wine and cook over a high heat, stirring occasionally, until reduced by half. Add the tomatoes, tomato purée and sugar and cook for a further 5 minutes. Pour in just enough water to cover and bring to the boil. Lower the heat, cover and simmer gently for 1 hour, until the duck is cooked through and tender.

Remove the saucepan from the heat and transfer the duck to a chopping board. Skim off the fat from the surface of the sauce and discard the bay leaf. Remove and discard the skin from the duck and cut the meat off the bones, then dice. Return the duck meat to the pan and keep warm.

Bring a large pan of salted water to the boil. Add the pasta, return to the boil and cook for 8–10 minutes, until tender but still firm to the bite. Drain and place in a serving dish. Spoon the sauce over the pasta and serve with Parmesan.

SERVES 4

4 tbsp olive oil

4 duck legs

1 shallot, finely chopped

1 leek, white part only, finely chopped

1 garlic clove, finely chopped

1 celery stick, finely chopped

1 carrot, finely chopped

4 pancetta or bacon slices, diced

1 tbsp finely chopped fresh flat-leaf parsley

1 bay leaf

5 tbsp dry white wine

400 g/14 oz canned chopped tomatoes

2 tbsp tomato purée

pinch of sugar

450 g/1 lb dried fettuccine

salt and pepper

freshly grated Parmesan cheese, to serve

FISH & SEAFOOD

SPAGHETTI ALLA PUTTANESCA

Heat the oil in a heavy-based frying pan. Add the garlic and cook over a low heat, stirring frequently, for 2 minutes. Add the anchovies and mash them to a pulp with a fork. Add the olives, capers and tomatoes and season to taste with cayenne pepper. Cover and simmer for 25 minutes.

Meanwhile, bring a large heavy-based saucepan of lightly salted water to the boil. Add the pasta, return to the boil and cook for 8–10 minutes, or until tender but still firm to the bite. Drain well and transfer to a warmed serving dish.

Spoon the anchovy sauce into the dish and toss the pasta, using 2 large forks. Garnish with the chopped parsley and serve immediately.

SERVES 4

3 tbsp olive oil

2 garlic cloves, finely chopped

10 canned anchovy fillets, drained and chopped

140 g/5 oz black olives, stoned and chopped

1 tbsp capers, drained and rinsed

450 g/1 lb plum tomatoes, peeled, deseeded and chopped

pinch of cayenne pepper

400 g/14 oz dried spaghetti

salt

2 tbsp chopped fresh parsley, to garnish

PENNE WITH SICILIAN SAUCE

Soak the sultanas in a bowl of warm water for about 20 minutes. Drain the sultanas thoroughly.

Preheat the grill, then cook the tomatoes under the hot grill for 10 minutes. Leave to cool slightly, then once cool enough to handle, peel off the skin and dice the flesh. Place the pine kernels on a baking tray and lightly toast under the grill for 2–3 minutes, or until golden brown.

Place the tomatoes, pine kernels and sultanas in a small saucepan and heat gently. Add the anchovies and tomato purée, and cook the sauce over a low heat for a further 2–3 minutes, or until hot.

Meanwhile, bring a large heavy-based saucepan of lightly salted water to the boil. Add the pasta, return to the boil and cook for 8–10 minutes, or until tender but still firm to the bite. Drain thoroughly, then transfer the pasta to a serving plate and serve with the Sicilian sauce.

SERVES 4

50 g/1¾ oz sultanas

450 g/1 lb tomatoes, halved

25 g/1 oz pine kernels

50 g/1¾ oz canned anchovies, drained and halved lengthways

2 tbsp tomato purée

350 g/12 oz dried penne

salt

SPINACH & ANCHOVY PASTA

Trim off any tough spinach stalks. Rinse the spinach leaves under cold running water and place them in a large saucepan with only the water that is clinging to them after washing. Cover and cook over a high heat, shaking the saucepan from time to time, until the spinach has wilted, but retains its colour. Drain well, reserve and keep warm.

Bring a large heavy-based saucepan of lightly salted water to the boil. Add the pasta, return to the boil and cook for 8–10 minutes, or until tender but still firm to the bite.

Heat 4 tablespoons of the oil in a separate saucepan. Add the pine kernels and cook until golden. Remove the pine kernels from the saucepan and reserve until required.

Add the garlic to the saucepan and cook until golden. Add the anchovies and stir in the spinach. Cook, stirring, for 2–3 minutes, until heated through. Return the pine kernels to the saucepan.

Drain the pasta, toss in the remaining oil and transfer to a warmed serving dish. Spoon the anchovy and spinach sauce over the pasta, toss lightly and serve immediately.

SERVES 4

900 g/2 lb fresh, young spinach leaves

400 g/14 oz dried fettuccine

5 tbsp olive oil

3 tbsp pine kernels

3 garlic cloves, crushed

8 canned anchovy fillets, drained and chopped

salt

GNOCCHI WITH TUNA, CAPERS & OLIVES

Bring a large saucepan of lightly salted water to the boil. Add the pasta, bring back to the boil and cook for 8–10 minutes, or until tender but still firm to the bite. Drain and return to the pan.

Heat the oil and half the butter in a frying pan over a medium–low heat. Add the garlic and cook for a few seconds until just beginning to colour. Reduce the heat to low. Add the tuna, lemon juice, capers and olives. Stir gently until all the ingredients are heated through.

Transfer the pasta to a warmed serving dish. Pour the tuna mixture over the pasta. Add the parsley and remaining butter. Toss well to mix. Serve immediately.

SERVES 4

350 g/12 oz dried gnocchi pasta

4 tbsp olive oil

4 tbsp butter

3 large garlic cloves, thinly sliced

200 g/7 oz canned tuna, drained and broken into chunks

2 tbsp lemon juice

1 tbsp capers, drained

10–12 black olives, stoned and sliced

salt

2 tbsp chopped fresh flat-leaf parsley, to serve

LINGUINE WITH SARDINES

Wash the sardine fillets and pat dry on kitchen paper. Roughly chop them into large pieces and reserve. Trim the fennel bulb, discard the outer leaves and slice very thinly.

Heat 2 tablespoons of the oil in a large frying pan over a medium–high heat and add the garlic and chillies. Cook for 1 minute, then add the fennel slices. Cook, stirring occasionally, for 4–5 minutes, or until softened. Reduce the heat, add the sardine pieces and cook for a further 3–4 minutes.

Meanwhile, bring a large pan of lightly salted water to the boil over a medium heat. Add the pasta and cook for 8–10 minutes, or until tender but still firm to the bite. Drain thoroughly and return to the pan.

Add the lemon rind, lemon juice, pine kernels and parsley to the sardine mixture and toss together. Season to taste with salt and pepper. Add to the pasta with the remaining oil and toss together gently. Transfer to a warmed serving dish and serve immediately.

SERVES 4

8 sardines, filleted

1 fennel bulb

4 tbsp olive oil

3 garlic cloves, sliced

1 tsp crushed chillies

350 g/12 oz dried linguine

½ tsp finely grated lemon rind

1 tbsp lemon juice

2 tbsp pine kernels, toasted

2 tbsp chopped fresh parsley

salt and pepper

FUSILLI WITH SMOKED SALMON & DILL

Bring a large heavy-based saucepan of lightly salted water to the boil. Add the pasta, return to the boil and cook for 8–10 minutes, or until tender but still firm to the bite.

Meanwhile, melt the butter in a heavy-based saucepan. Add the onion and cook over a low heat, stirring occasionally, for 5 minutes, or until softened. Add the wine, bring to the boil and continue boiling until reduced by two thirds. Pour in the cream and season to taste with salt and pepper. Bring to the boil, reduce the heat and simmer for 2 minutes, or until slightly thickened. Cut the smoked salmon into squares and stir into the saucepan with the snipped dill and lemon juice to taste.

Drain the pasta and transfer to a warmed serving dish. Add the smoked salmon mixture, toss well, garnish with dill sprigs and serve immediately.

SERVES 4

450 g/1 lb dried fusilli

55 g/2 oz unsalted butter

1 small onion, finely chopped

6 tbsp dry white wine

425 ml/15 fl oz double cream

225 g/8 oz smoked salmon

2 tbsp snipped fresh dill, plus extra sprigs to garnish

1–2 tbsp lemon juice

salt and pepper

FETTUCCINE ALLA BUCANIERA

Spread the flour out on a plate and season with salt and pepper. Coat all the fish pieces with it, shaking off the excess. Melt the butter in a heavy-based saucepan or flameproof casserole. Add the fish, shallots, garlic, carrot and leek, then cook over a low heat, stirring frequently, for 10 minutes. Sprinkle in any remaining seasoned flour and cook, stirring constantly, for 1 minute.

Mix the stock, wine, anchovy essence and vinegar together in a jug and gradually stir into the fish mixture. Bring to the boil, stirring constantly, then reduce the heat and simmer gently for 15 minutes.

Meanwhile, bring a large heavy-based saucepan of lightly salted water to the boil. Add the pasta, return to the boil and cook for 8–10 minutes, or until tender but still firm to the bite. Drain and transfer to a warmed serving dish. Spoon the fish mixture onto the pasta, garnish with chopped parsley and serve immediately.

SERVES 6

1 tbsp plain flour

450 g/1 lb lemon sole fillets, skinned and cut into chunks

450 g/1 lb monkfish fillets, skinned and cut into chunks

85 g/3 oz unsalted butter

4 shallots, finely chopped

2 garlic cloves, crushed

1 carrot, diced

1 leek, finely chopped

300 ml/10 fl oz fish stock

300 ml/10 fl oz dry white wine

2 tsp anchovy essence

1 tbsp balsamic vinegar

450 g/1 lb dried fettuccine

salt and pepper

chopped fresh flat-leaf parsley, to garnish

FUSILLI WITH MONKFISH & BROCCOLI

Divide the broccoli florets into tiny sprigs. Bring a saucepan of lightly salted water to the boil, add the broccoli and cook for 2 minutes. Drain and refresh under cold running water.

Heat the oil in a large heavy-based frying pan. Add the monkfish and garlic and season to taste with salt and pepper. Cook, stirring frequently, for 5 minutes, or until the fish is opaque. Pour in the white wine and cream and cook, stirring occasionally, for 5 minutes, or until the fish is cooked through and the sauce has thickened. Stir in the broccoli florets.

Meanwhile, bring a large heavy-based saucepan of lightly salted water to the boil. Add the pasta, return to the boil and cook for 8–10 minutes, or until tender but still firm to the bite. Drain the pasta and tip into the saucepan with the fish, add the Gorgonzola cheese and toss lightly. Serve immediately.

SERVES 4

115 g/4 oz broccoli, divided into florets

3 tbsp olive oil

350 g/12 oz monkfish fillet, skinned and cut into bite-sized pieces

2 garlic cloves, crushed

125 ml/4 fl oz dry white wine

225 ml/8 fl oz double cream

400 g/14 oz dried fusilli

85 g/3 oz Gorgonzola cheese, diced

salt and pepper

SPRINGTIME PASTA

Fill a bowl with cold water and add the lemon juice. Prepare the artichokes one at a time. Cut off the stems and trim away any tough outer leaves. Cut across the tops of the leaves. Slice in half lengthways and remove the central fibrous chokes, then cut lengthways into 5 mm/¼ inch thick slices. Immediately place the slices in the bowl of acidulated water to prevent discoloration.

Heat 5 tablespoons of the oil in a heavy-based frying pan. Drain the artichoke slices and pat dry with kitchen paper. Add them to the frying pan with the shallots, garlic, parsley and mint and cook over a low heat, stirring frequently, for 10–12 minutes, until tender.

Meanwhile, bring a large saucepan of lightly salted water to the boil. Add the pasta, bring back to the boil and cook for 8–10 minutes, until tender but still firm to the bite.

Peel the prawns, cut a slit along the back of each and remove and discard the dark vein. Melt the butter in a small frying pan and add the prawns. Cook, stirring occasionally, for 2–3 minutes, until they have changed colour. Season to taste with salt and pepper.

Drain the pasta and tip it into a bowl. Add the remaining oil and toss well. Add the artichoke mixture and the prawns and toss again. Serve immediately.

SERVES 4

2 tbsp lemon juice

4 baby globe artichokes

7 tbsp olive oil

2 shallots, finely chopped

2 garlic cloves, finely chopped

2 tbsp chopped fresh flat-leaf parsley

2 tbsp chopped fresh mint

350 g/12 oz dried rigatoni

12 large raw prawns

25 g/1 oz unsalted butter

salt and pepper

TAGLIATELLE
IN A CREAMY
PRAWN SAUCE

Heat the oil and butter in a saucepan over a medium–low heat. Add the garlic and red pepper. Cook for a few seconds until the garlic is just beginning to colour. Stir in the tomato purée and wine. Cook for 10 minutes, stirring.

Bring a large saucepan of lightly salted water to the boil. Add the pasta, bring back to the boil and cook for 8–10 minutes, or until tender but still firm to the bite. Drain and return to the pan.

Add the prawns to the sauce and increase the heat to medium–high. Cook for 2 minutes, stirring, until the prawns turn pink. Reduce the heat and stir in the cream. Cook for 1 minute, stirring constantly, until thickened. Season to taste with salt and pepper.

Transfer the pasta to a warmed serving dish. Pour the sauce over the pasta. Sprinkle with the parsley. Toss well to mix and serve immediately.

SERVES 4

3 tbsp olive oil

3 tbsp butter

4 garlic cloves, very finely chopped

2 tbsp finely diced red pepper

2 tbsp tomato purée

125 ml/4 fl oz dry white wine

450 g/1 lb dried tagliatelle

350 g/12 oz raw peeled prawns

125 ml/4 fl oz double cream

salt and pepper

3 tbsp chopped fresh flat-leaf parsley, to garnish

LINGUINE WITH PRAWNS & SCALLOPS

Peel and devein the prawns, reserving the shells. Melt the butter in a heavy-based frying pan. Add the shallots and cook over a low heat, stirring occasionally, for 5 minutes, or until softened. Add the prawn shells and cook, stirring constantly, for 1 minute. Pour in the vermouth and cook, stirring, for 1 minute. Add the water, bring to the boil, then reduce the heat and simmer for 10 minutes, or until the liquid has reduced by half. Remove the frying pan from the heat.

Bring a large heavy-based saucepan of lightly salted water to the boil. Add the pasta, return to the boil and cook for 8–10 minutes, or until tender but still firm to the bite.

Meanwhile, heat the oil in a separate heavy-based frying pan. Add the scallops and prawns and cook, stirring frequently, for 2 minutes, or until the scallops are opaque and the prawns have changed colour. Strain the prawn-shell stock into the frying pan. Drain the pasta and add to the frying pan with the chives and season to taste with salt and pepper. Toss well over a low heat for 1 minute, then serve.

SERVES 6

450 g/1 lb raw prawns

25 g/1 oz butter

2 shallots, finely chopped

225 ml/8 fl oz dry white vermouth

350 ml/12 fl oz water

450 g/1 lb dried linguine

2 tbsp olive oil

450 g/1 lb prepared scallops, thawed if frozen

2 tbsp snipped fresh chives

salt and pepper

LINGUINE WITH MIXED SEAFOOD

Heat the oil in a saucepan. Add the shallots, garlic and chilli and cook over a low heat, stirring occasionally, for 5 minutes. Increase the heat to medium, stir in the tomatoes, parsley and sugar and season to taste with salt and pepper. Bring to the boil, then cover and simmer, stirring occasionally, for 15–20 minutes.

Discard any mussels or clams with broken shells or any that refuse to close when tapped. Pour the wine into a large saucepan and add the lemon slices, mussels and clams. Cover and cook over a high heat, shaking the pan occasionally, for 5 minutes, until all the shellfish have opened. Using a slotted spoon, transfer the shellfish to a bowl and reserve the cooking liquid.

Discard any mussels and clams that remain closed. Reserve a few for the garnish and remove the remainder from their shells. Strain the cooking liquid through a muslin-lined sieve.

Bring a saucepan of lightly salted water to the boil. Add the pasta and cook for 8–10 minutes, until tender but still firm to the bite.

Meanwhile, stir the strained cooking liquid into the shallot and tomato mixture and bring to the boil, stirring constantly. Add the shelled mussels and clams and the prawns. Taste and adjust the seasoning, if necessary, and heat through gently.

Strain the pasta and return it to the pan. Add the shellfish mixture and toss well. Serve, garnished with the reserved shellfish and parsley sprigs.

SERVES 4–6

2 tbsp olive oil

2 shallots, finely chopped

2 garlic cloves, finely chopped

1 small red chilli, deseeded and finely chopped

200 g/7 oz canned chopped tomatoes

½ bunch fresh flat-leaf parsley, chopped, plus extra sprigs to garnish

pinch of sugar

450 g/1 lb live mussels, scrubbed and debearded

450 g/1 lb live clams, scrubbed

6 tbsp dry white wine

1 lemon, sliced

450 g/1 lb dried linguine

175 g/6 oz large cooked prawns, shelled and deveined

salt and pepper

PAPPARDELLE WITH SCALLOPS & PORCINI

Put the porcini and hot water in a bowl. Leave to soak for 20 minutes. Strain the mushrooms, reserving the soaking water, and chop roughly. Line a sieve with two pieces of kitchen paper and strain the mushroom water into a bowl.

Heat the oil and butter in a large frying pan over a medium heat. Add the scallops and cook for 2 minutes until just golden. Add the garlic and mushrooms, then cook for another minute.

Stir in the lemon juice, cream and 125 ml/4 fl oz of the mushroom water. Bring to the boil, then simmer over a medium heat for 2–3 minutes, stirring constantly, until the liquid is reduced by half. Season to taste with salt and pepper. Remove from the heat.

Bring a large saucepan of lightly salted water to the boil. Add the pasta, bring back to the boil and cook for 8–10 minutes, or until tender but still firm to the bite. Drain and transfer to a warmed serving dish. Briefly reheat the sauce and pour over the pasta. Sprinkle with the parsley and toss well to mix. Serve immediately.

SERVES 4

25 g/1 oz dried porcini mushrooms

500 ml/18 fl oz hot water

3 tbsp olive oil

3 tbsp butter

350 g/12 oz scallops, sliced

2 garlic cloves, very finely chopped

2 tbsp lemon juice

250 ml/9 fl oz double cream

350 g/12 oz dried pappardelle

salt and pepper

2 tbsp chopped fresh flat-leaf parsley, to serve

SPAGHETTI CON VONGOLE

Discard any clams with broken shells or any that refuse to close when tapped. Place the clams in a large heavy-based saucepan. Add the water and wine, then cover and cook over a high heat, shaking the saucepan occasionally, for 5 minutes, or until the shells have opened. Remove the clams with a slotted spoon and strain the liquid through a muslin-lined sieve into a small saucepan. Bring to the boil and cook until reduced by about half. Discard any clams that remain closed and remove the remainder from their shells.

Bring a large heavy-based saucepan of lightly salted water to the boil. Add the pasta, return to the boil and cook for 8–10 minutes, or until tender but still firm to the bite.

Meanwhile, heat the oil in a large heavy-based frying pan. Add the garlic and cook, stirring frequently, for 2 minutes. Add the parsley and the reduced cooking liquid and simmer gently. Drain the pasta and add it to the frying pan with the clams. Season to taste with salt and pepper and cook, stirring constantly, for 4 minutes, or until the pasta is coated and the clams have heated through. Transfer to a warmed serving dish and serve immediately.

SERVES 4

1 kg/2 lb 4 oz live clams, scrubbed

175 ml/6 fl oz water

175 ml/6 fl oz dry white wine

350 g/12 oz dried spaghetti

5 tbsp olive oil

2 garlic cloves, finely chopped

4 tbsp chopped fresh flat-leaf parsley

salt and pepper

CONCHIGLIE
WITH MUSSELS

Discard any mussels with broken shells or any that refuse to close when tapped. Place the mussels in a large heavy-based saucepan, together with the wine and half of the onions. Cover and cook over a medium heat, shaking the saucepan frequently, for 2–3 minutes, or until the shells open. Remove the saucepan from the heat. Drain the mussels and reserve the cooking liquid. Discard any mussels that remain closed. Strain the cooking liquid through a muslin-lined sieve into a bowl and reserve.

Melt the butter in a saucepan. Add the remaining onions and cook until translucent. Stir in the garlic and cook for 1 minute. Gradually stir in the reserved cooking liquid. Stir in the parsley and cream and season to taste with salt and pepper. Bring to simmering point over a low heat.

Meanwhile, bring a large saucepan of lightly salted water to the boil. Add the pasta and cook for 8–10 minutes, or until tender but still firm to the bite. Drain and keep warm.

Reserve a few mussels for the garnish and remove the remainder from their shells. Stir the shelled mussels into the cream sauce and warm briefly. Transfer the pasta to a serving dish. Pour over the sauce and toss to coat. Garnish with the reserved mussels and serve.

SERVES 6

1.25 kg/2 lb 12 oz live mussels, scrubbed and debearded

225 ml/8 fl oz dry white wine

2 large onions, chopped

115 g/4 oz unsalted butter

6 large garlic cloves, finely chopped

5 tbsp chopped fresh parsley

300 ml/10 fl oz double cream

400 g/14 oz dried conchiglie

salt and pepper

SPAGHETTI WITH CRAB

Using a sharp knife, scoop the meat from the crab shell into a bowl. Mix the white and brown meat together lightly and reserve.

Bring a large pan of lightly salted water to the boil over a medium heat. Add the pasta and cook for 8–10 minutes, or until tender but still firm to the bite. Drain thoroughly and return to the pan.

Meanwhile, heat 2 tablespoons of the oil in a frying pan over a low heat. Add the chilli and garlic and cook for 30 seconds, then add the crabmeat, parsley, lemon juice and lemon rind. Cook for 1 minute, until the crab is just heated through.

Add the crab mixture to the pasta with the remaining oil and season to taste with salt and pepper. Toss together thoroughly, transfer to a large warmed serving dish and garnish with lemon wedges. Serve immediately.

SERVES 4

1 dressed crab, about 450 g/ 1 lb including the shell

350 g/12 oz dried spaghetti

6 tbsp extra virgin olive oil

1 fresh red chilli, deseeded and finely chopped

2 garlic cloves, finely chopped

3 tbsp chopped fresh parsley

2 tbsp lemon juice

1 tsp finely grated lemon rind

salt and pepper

lemon wedges, to garnish

PENNE WITH SQUID & TOMATOES

Bring a large heavy-based saucepan of lightly salted water to the boil. Add the pasta, return to the boil and cook for 3 minutes, then drain and reserve until required. With a sharp knife, cut the squid into strips.

Heat the oil in a large saucepan. Add the onions and cook over a low heat, stirring occasionally, for 5 minutes, or until softened. Add the squid and stock, bring to the boil and simmer for 3 minutes. Stir in the wine, tomatoes and their can juices, tomato purée, marjoram and bay leaf. Season to taste with salt and pepper. Bring to the boil and cook for 5 minutes, or until slightly reduced.

Add the pasta, return to the boil and simmer for 5–7 minutes, or until tender but still firm to the bite. Remove and discard the bay leaf. Transfer to a warmed serving dish, garnish with the parsley and serve immediately.

SERVES 4

225 g/8 oz dried penne

350 g/12 oz prepared squid

6 tbsp olive oil

2 onions, sliced

225 ml/8 fl oz fish or chicken stock

150 ml/5 fl oz full-bodied red wine

400 g/14 oz canned chopped tomatoes

2 tbsp tomato purée

1 tbsp chopped fresh marjoram

1 bay leaf

salt and pepper

2 tbsp chopped fresh parsley, to garnish

VEGETARIAN

SPAGHETTI OLIO E AGLIO

VEGETARIAN

Bring a large heavy-based saucepan of lightly salted water to the boil. Add the pasta, return to the boil and cook for 8–10 minutes, or until tender but still firm to the bite.

Meanwhile, heat the oil in a heavy-based frying pan. Add the garlic and a pinch of salt and cook over a low heat, stirring constantly, for 3–4 minutes, or until golden. Do not allow the garlic to brown or it will taste bitter. Remove the frying pan from the heat.

Drain the pasta and transfer to a warmed serving dish. Pour in the garlic-flavoured oil, then add the chopped parsley and season to taste with salt and pepper. Toss well and serve immediately.

SERVES 4

450 g/1 lb dried spaghetti

125 ml/4 fl oz extra virgin olive oil

3 garlic cloves, finely chopped

3 tbsp chopped fresh flat-leaf parsley

salt and pepper

CREAMY PAPPARDELLE
WITH BROCCOLI

Melt half the butter in a large pan over a medium heat. Add the onion and cook for 4 minutes.

Add the pasta and broccoli to the pan and cook, stirring constantly, for 2 minutes. Add the stock, bring back to the boil and simmer for 8–10 minutes. Season well with salt and white pepper.

Meanwhile, melt the remaining butter in a pan over a medium heat. Sprinkle over the flour and cook, stirring constantly, for 2 minutes. Gradually stir in the cream and bring to simmering point, but do not boil. Add the mozzarella cheese and season to taste with salt, white pepper and a little freshly grated nutmeg.

Drain the pasta and broccoli mixture and return to the pan. Pour over the cheese sauce. Cook, stirring occasionally, for 2 minutes. Transfer the pasta and broccoli mixture to a large warmed serving dish and garnish with a few slices of apple. Serve immediately.

SERVES 4

55 g/2 oz butter

1 large onion, finely chopped

450 g/1 lb dried pappardelle

450 g/1 lb broccoli, broken into florets

150 ml/5 fl oz vegetable stock

1 tbsp plain flour

150 ml/5 fl oz single cream

55 g/2 oz freshly grated mozzarella cheese

freshly grated nutmeg

salt and white pepper

fresh apple slices, to garnish

PENNE WITH ASPARAGUS & GORGONZOLA

Preheat the oven to 230°C/450°F/Gas Mark 8. Place the asparagus tips in a single layer in a shallow ovenproof dish. Sprinkle with the oil and season to taste with salt and pepper. Turn to coat in the oil and seasoning. Roast in the preheated oven for 10–12 minutes until slightly browned and just tender. Set aside and keep warm.

Combine the crumbled cheese with the cream in a bowl. Season to taste with salt and pepper.

Bring a large saucepan of lightly salted water to a boil. Add the pasta, bring back to a boil and cook for 8–10 minutes, or until tender but still firm to the bite. Drain and transfer to a warmed serving dish. Immediately add the asparagus and the cheese mixture. Toss well until the cheese has melted and the pasta is coated with the sauce. Serve immediately.

SERVES 4

450 g/1 lb asparagus tips

1 tbsp olive oil

225 g/8 oz Gorgonzola cheese, crumbled

175 ml/6 fl oz double cream

350 g/12 oz dried penne

salt and pepper

RIGATONI WITH PEPPERS & GOAT'S CHEESE

Heat the oil and butter in a large frying pan over a medium heat. Add the onion and cook until soft. Increase the heat to medium–high and add the peppers and garlic. Cook for 12–15 minutes, stirring, until the peppers are tender but not mushy. Season to taste with salt and pepper. Remove from the heat.

Bring a large saucepan of lightly salted water to the boil. Add the pasta, bring back to the boil and cook for 8–10 minutes, or until tender but still firm to the bite. Drain and transfer to a warmed serving dish. Add the goat's cheese and toss to mix.

Briefly reheat the sauce. Add the basil and olives. Pour over the pasta and toss well to mix. Serve immediately.

SERVES 4

2 tbsp olive oil

1 tbsp butter

1 small onion, finely chopped

4 peppers, yellow and red, deseeded and cut into 2-cm/³⁄₄-inch squares

3 garlic cloves, thinly sliced

450 g/1 lb dried rigatoni

125 g/4¹⁄₂ oz goat's cheese, crumbled

15 fresh basil leaves, shredded

10 black olives, stoned and sliced

salt and pepper

PENNE WITH CREAMY MUSHROOMS

Melt the butter with the oil in a large heavy-based frying pan. Add the shallots and cook over a low heat, stirring occasionally, for 4–5 minutes, or until softened. Add the mushrooms and cook over a low heat for a further 2 minutes. Season to taste with salt and pepper, sprinkle in the flour and cook, stirring, for 1 minute.

Remove the frying pan from the heat and gradually stir in the cream and port. Return to the heat, add the sun-dried tomatoes and grated nutmeg and cook over a low heat, stirring occasionally, for 8 minutes.

Meanwhile, bring a large heavy-based saucepan of lightly salted water to the boil. Add the pasta, return to the boil and cook for 8–10 minutes, or until tender but still firm to the bite. Drain the pasta well and add to the mushroom sauce. Cook for 3 minutes, then transfer to a warmed serving dish. Sprinkle with the chopped parsley and serve immediately.

SERVES 4

55 g/2 oz butter

1 tbsp olive oil

6 shallots, sliced

450 g/1 lb chestnut mushrooms, sliced

1 tsp plain flour

150 ml/5 fl oz double cream

2 tbsp port

115 g/4 oz sun-dried tomatoes in oil, drained and chopped

pinch of freshly grated nutmeg

350 g/12 oz dried penne

salt and pepper

2 tbsp chopped fresh flat-leaf parsley, to garnish

TAGLIATELLE WITH WALNUT SAUCE

Place the breadcrumbs, walnuts, garlic, milk, oil and fromage frais in a large mortar and grind to a smooth paste with a pestle. Alternatively, place the ingredients in a food processor and process until smooth. Stir in the cream to give a thick sauce consistency and season to taste with salt and pepper. Reserve.

Bring a large heavy-based saucepan of lightly salted water to the boil. Add the pasta, return to the boil and cook for 8–10 minutes, or until tender but still firm to the bite.

Drain the pasta and transfer to a warmed serving dish. Add the walnut sauce and toss thoroughly to coat. Serve immediately.

SERVES 4

25 g/1 oz fresh white breadcrumbs

350 g/12 oz walnut pieces

2 garlic cloves, finely chopped

4 tbsp milk

4 tbsp olive oil

85 g/3 oz fromage frais or cream cheese

150 ml/5 fl oz single cream

350 g/12 oz dried tagliatelle

salt and pepper

TAGLIATELLE
WITH GARLIC
CRUMBS

Mix the breadcrumbs, parsley, chives and marjoram together in a small bowl.

Heat the oil in a large heavy-based frying pan. Add the breadcrumb mixture and the garlic and pine kernels, season to taste with salt and pepper and cook over a low heat, stirring constantly, for 5 minutes, or until the breadcrumbs become golden, but not crisp. Remove the frying pan from the heat and cover to keep warm.

Bring a large heavy-based saucepan of lightly salted water to the boil. Add the pasta, return to the boil and cook for 8–10 minutes, or until tender but still firm to the bite.

Drain the pasta and transfer to a warmed serving dish. Drizzle with a little oil and toss to mix. Add the garlic breadcrumbs and toss again. Serve immediately with the grated pecorino cheese.

SERVES 4

350 g/12 oz fresh white breadcrumbs

4 tbsp finely chopped fresh flat-leaf parsley

1 tbsp snipped fresh chives

2 tbsp finely chopped fresh marjoram

3 tbsp olive oil, plus extra to serve

3–4 garlic cloves, finely chopped

55 g/2 oz pine kernels

450 g/1 lb dried tagliatelle, preferably a mixture of green and white

salt and pepper

55 g/2 oz freshly grated pecorino cheese, to serve

NEAPOLITAN
CONCHIGLIE

Place the tomatoes in a large heavy-based saucepan. Add the wine, onion, carrot, celery, parsley and sugar and gradually bring to the boil, stirring frequently. Reduce the heat, partially cover and simmer, stirring occasionally, for 45 minutes, or until thickened.

Meanwhile, bring a large heavy-based saucepan of lightly salted water to the boil. Add the pasta, return to the boil and cook for 8–10 minutes, or until tender but still firm to the bite.

Rub the tomato sauce through a sieve with the back of a wooden spoon into a clean saucepan and stir in the marjoram. Reheat gently, stirring occasionally, for 1–2 minutes. Drain the pasta and transfer to a warmed serving dish. Pour the tomato sauce over the pasta and toss well. Sprinkle with Parmesan cheese and serve immediately.

SERVES 4

900 g/2 lb plum tomatoes, roughly chopped

150 ml/5 fl oz dry white wine

1 onion, chopped

1 carrot, chopped

1 celery stick, chopped

2 fresh flat-leaf parsley sprigs

pinch of sugar

350 g/12 oz dried conchiglie

1 tbsp chopped fresh marjoram

salt

freshly grated Parmesan cheese, to serve

FUSILLI WITH SUN-DRIED TOMATOES

Put the sun-dried tomatoes in a bowl, pour over the boiling water and leave to stand for 5 minutes. Using a slotted spoon, remove one third of the tomatoes from the bowl. Cut into bite-sized pieces. Put the remaining tomatoes and water into a blender and purée.

Heat the oil in a large frying pan over a medium heat. Add the onion and cook gently for 5 minutes, or until soft. Add the garlic and cook until just beginning to colour. Add the puréed tomato and the reserved tomato pieces to the pan. Bring to the boil, then simmer over a medium–low heat for 10 minutes. Stir in the herbs and season to taste with salt and pepper. Simmer for 1 minute, then remove from the heat.

Bring a large saucepan of lightly salted water to the boil. Add the pasta, bring back to the boil and cook for 8–10 minutes, or until tender but still firm to the bite. Drain and transfer to a warmed serving dish. Briefly reheat the sauce. Pour over the pasta, add the basil and toss well to mix. Sprinkle with the Parmesan cheese and serve immediately.

SERVES 4

85 g/3 oz sun-dried tomatoes (not in oil)

700 ml/1¼ pints boiling water

2 tbsp olive oil

1 onion, finely chopped

2 large garlic cloves, finely sliced

2 tbsp chopped fresh flat-leaf parsley

2 tsp chopped fresh oregano

1 tsp chopped fresh rosemary

350 g/12 oz dried fusilli

10 fresh basil leaves, shredded

salt and pepper

freshly grated Parmesan cheese, to serve

FETTUCCINE
WITH OLIVES & PEPPERS

Heat the oil in a large heavy-based saucepan. Add the onion and cook over a low heat, stirring occasionally, for 5 minutes, or until softened. Add the olives, tomatoes and peppers and season to taste with salt and pepper. Cover and simmer gently over a very low heat, stirring occasionally, for 35 minutes.

Meanwhile, bring a large heavy-based saucepan of lightly salted water to the boil. Add the pasta, return to the boil and cook for 8–10 minutes, or until tender but still firm to the bite. Drain the pasta and transfer to a warmed serving dish.

Spoon the sauce onto the pasta and toss well. Serve immediately with the grated pecorino cheese.

SERVES 4

100 ml/3½ fl oz olive oil

1 onion, finely chopped

200 g/7 oz black olives, stoned and roughly chopped

400 g/14 oz canned chopped tomatoes, drained

2 red, yellow or orange peppers, deseeded and cut into thin strips

350 g/12 oz dried fettuccine

salt and pepper

freshly grated pecorino cheese, to serve

OLIVE, PEPPER & CHERRY TOMATO PASTA

Bring a large heavy-based saucepan of lightly salted water to the boil. Add the pasta, return to the boil and cook for 8–10 minutes, or until tender but still firm to the bite. Drain the pasta thoroughly.

Heat the oil and butter in a frying pan until the butter melts. Sauté the garlic for 30 seconds. Add the peppers and cook, stirring constantly, for 3–4 minutes.

Stir in the cherry tomatoes, oregano, wine and olives and cook for 3–4 minutes. Season well with salt and pepper and stir in the rocket until just wilted. Transfer the pasta to a serving dish, spoon over the sauce and garnish with oregano sprigs. Serve.

SERVES 4

225 g/8 oz dried penne

2 tbsp olive oil

25 g/1 oz butter

2 garlic cloves, crushed

1 green pepper, deseeded and thinly sliced

1 yellow pepper, deseeded and thinly sliced

16 cherry tomatoes, halved

1 tbsp chopped fresh oregano, plus extra sprigs to garnish

125 ml/4 fl oz dry white wine

2 tbsp quartered, stoned black olives

75 g/2¾ oz rocket

salt and pepper

SPAGHETTI
ALLA NORMA

Heat 4 tablespoons of the oil in a large saucepan. Add the tomatoes and garlic, season to taste with salt and pepper, cover and cook over a low heat, stirring occasionally, for 25 minutes.

Meanwhile, heat the remaining oil in a heavy-based frying pan. Add the aubergines and cook, stirring occasionally, for 5 minutes, until evenly golden brown. Remove with a slotted spoon and drain on kitchen paper.

Bring a large pan of salted water to the boil. Add the pasta, bring back to the boil and cook for 8–10 minutes, until tender but still firm to the bite.

Meanwhile, stir the drained aubergines into the tomato mixture. Taste and adjust the seasoning, if necessary.

Drain the pasta and place in a warmed serving dish. Add the tomato and aubergine mixture, basil and half the pecorino cheese. Toss well, sprinkle with the remaining cheese and serve immediately.

SERVES 4

175 ml/6 fl oz olive oil

500 g/1 lb 2 oz plum tomatoes, peeled and chopped

1 garlic clove, chopped

350 g/12 oz aubergines, diced

400 g/14 oz dried spaghetti

½ bunch fresh basil, torn

115 g/4 oz freshly grated pecorino cheese

salt and pepper

FARFALLE WITH AUBERGINES

Place the aubergine in a colander, sprinkling each layer with salt, and leave to drain for 30 minutes. Meanwhile, heat 1 tablespoon of the oil in a heavy-based saucepan. Add the shallots and garlic and cook over a low heat, stirring occasionally, for 5 minutes, or until softened. Add the tomatoes and their can juices, stir in the sugar and season to taste with salt and pepper. Cover and simmer gently, stirring occasionally, for 30 minutes, or until thickened.

Rinse the aubergine under cold running water, drain well and pat dry with kitchen paper. Heat half the remaining oil in a heavy-based frying pan, then add the aubergine in batches, and cook, stirring frequently, until golden brown all over. Remove from the frying pan with a slotted spoon and keep warm while you cook the remaining batches, adding the remaining oil as necessary.

Meanwhile, bring a large heavy-based saucepan of lightly salted water to the boil. Add the pasta, return to the boil and cook for 8–10 minutes, or until tender but still firm to the bite. Drain the pasta and transfer to a warmed serving dish.

Pour the tomato sauce over the pasta and toss well to mix. Top with the diced aubergine, garnish with fresh basil sprigs and serve.

SERVES 4

1 large or 2 medium aubergines, diced

150 ml/5 fl oz olive oil

4 shallots, chopped

2 garlic cloves, finely chopped

400 g/14 oz canned chopped tomatoes

1 tsp caster sugar

350 g/12 oz dried farfalle

salt and pepper

fresh basil sprigs, to garnish

VERMICELLI WITH VEGETABLE RIBBONS

Bring a large heavy-based saucepan of lightly salted water to the boil. Add the pasta, return to the boil and cook for 5 minutes, or until tender but still firm to the bite.

Meanwhile, cut the courgettes and carrots into very thin strips with a swivel-blade vegetable peeler or a mandolin. Melt the butter with the oil in a heavy-based frying pan. Add the carrot strips and garlic and cook over a low heat, stirring occasionally, for 5 minutes. Add the courgette strips and all the herbs and season to taste with salt and pepper.

Drain the pasta and add it to the frying pan. Toss well to mix and cook, stirring occasionally, for 5 minutes. Transfer to a warmed serving dish, add the radicchio, toss well and serve immediately.

SERVES 4

350 g/12 oz dried vermicelli

3 courgettes

3 carrots

25 g/1 oz unsalted butter

1 tbsp olive oil

2 garlic cloves, finely chopped

85 g/3 oz fresh basil, shredded

25 g/1 oz fresh chives, finely snipped

25 g/1 oz fresh flat-leaf parsley, finely chopped

1 small head radicchio, leaves shredded

salt and pepper

PASTA WITH GREEN VEGETABLES

Bring a large heavy-based saucepan of lightly salted water to the boil. Add the pasta, return to the boil and cook for 8–10 minutes, or until tender but still firm to the bite. Drain the pasta in a colander, return to the saucepan, cover and keep warm.

Steam the broccoli, courgettes, asparagus spears and mangetout over a saucepan of boiling, salted water until just beginning to soften. Remove from the heat and plunge into cold water to prevent further cooking. Drain and reserve. Cook the peas in boiling, salted water for 3 minutes, then drain. Refresh in cold water and drain again.

Place the butter and stock in a saucepan over a medium heat. Add all the vegetables except for the asparagus spears and toss carefully with a wooden spoon to heat through, taking care not to break them up. Stir in the cream, allow the sauce to heat through and season to taste with salt, pepper and nutmeg.

Transfer the pasta to a warmed serving dish and stir in the chopped parsley. Spoon the sauce over and arrange the asparagus spears on top. Sprinkle with the freshly grated Parmesan cheese and serve hot.

SERVES 4

225 g/8 oz dried fusilli

1 head broccoli, cut into florets

2 courgettes, sliced

225 g/8 oz asparagus spears, trimmed

125 g/4½ oz mangetout

125 g/4½ oz frozen peas

25 g/1 oz butter

3 tbsp vegetable stock

5 tbsp double cream

large pinch of freshly grated nutmeg

2 tbsp chopped fresh parsley

salt and pepper

2 tbsp freshly grated Parmesan cheese, to serve

PAPPARDELLE WITH PUMPKIN SAUCE

Melt the butter in a large heavy-based saucepan. Add the shallots, sprinkle with a little salt, cover and cook over a very low heat, stirring occasionally, for 30 minutes.

Add the pumpkin pieces and season to taste with nutmeg. Cover and cook over a very low heat, stirring occasionally, for 40 minutes, or until the pumpkin is pulpy. Stir in the cream, Parmesan cheese and parsley and remove the saucepan from the heat.

Meanwhile, bring a large heavy-based saucepan of lightly salted water to the boil. Add the pasta, return to the boil and cook for 8–10 minutes, or until tender but still firm to the bite. Drain, reserving 2–3 tablespoons of the cooking water.

Add the pasta to the pumpkin mixture and stir in the reserved cooking water if the mixture seems too thick. Cook, stirring, for 1 minute, then transfer to a warmed serving dish and serve immediately with extra grated Parmesan cheese.

SERVES 4

55 g/2 oz butter

6 shallots, very finely chopped

800 g/1 lb 12 oz pumpkin, peeled, deseeded and cut into pieces

pinch of freshly grated nutmeg

200 ml/7 fl oz single cream

4 tbsp freshly grated Parmesan cheese, plus extra to serve

2 tbsp chopped fresh flat-leaf parsley

350 g/12 oz dried pappardelle

salt

PENNE WITH MIXED BEANS

Heat the oil in a large heavy-based frying pan. Add the onion, garlic, carrot and celery and cook over a low heat, stirring occasionally, for 5 minutes, or until the onion has softened.

Add the mixed beans, passata and chopped chervil to the frying pan and season the mixture to taste with salt and pepper. Cover and simmer gently for 15 minutes.

Meanwhile, bring a large heavy-based saucepan of lightly salted water to the boil. Add the pasta, return to the boil and cook for 8–10 minutes, or until tender but still firm to the bite. Drain the pasta and transfer to a warmed serving dish. Add the mixed bean sauce, toss well and serve immediately, garnished with extra chervil.

SERVES 4

1 tbsp olive oil

1 onion, chopped

1 garlic clove, finely chopped

1 carrot, finely chopped

1 celery stick, finely chopped

425 g/15 oz canned mixed beans, drained and rinsed

225 ml/8 fl oz passata

1 tbsp chopped fresh chervil, plus extra leaves to garnish

350 g/12 oz dried penne

salt and pepper

FILLED & BAKED

LASAGNE AL FORNO

Preheat the oven to 190°C/375°F/Gas Mark 5. Heat the oil in a large heavy-based saucepan. Add the pancetta and cook over a medium heat, stirring occasionally, for 3 minutes, or until the fat begins to run. Add the onion and garlic and cook, stirring occasionally, for 5 minutes, or until softened.

Add the beef and cook, breaking it up with a wooden spoon, until browned all over. Stir in the celery and carrots and cook for 5 minutes. Season to taste with salt and pepper. Add the sugar, oregano and tomatoes and their can juices. Bring to the boil, reduce the heat and simmer for 30 minutes.

Meanwhile, to make the cheese sauce, stir the mustard and Cheddar cheese into the Béchamel Sauce.

In a large, rectangular ovenproof dish, make alternate layers of meat sauce, lasagne sheets and Parmesan cheese. Pour the cheese sauce over the layers, covering them completely, and sprinkle with Parmesan cheese. Bake in the preheated oven for 30 minutes, or until golden brown and bubbling. Serve immediately.

SERVES 4

2 tbsp olive oil

55 g/2 oz pancetta, chopped

1 onion, chopped

1 garlic clove, finely chopped

225 g/8 oz fresh beef mince

2 celery sticks, chopped

2 carrots, chopped

pinch of sugar

½ tsp dried oregano

400 g/14 oz canned chopped
   tomatoes

2 tsp Dijon mustard

140 g/5 oz Cheddar cheese, grated

300 ml/10 fl oz Béchamel Sauce
   (see page 7)

225 g/8 oz dried no pre-cook
   lasagne sheets

115 g/4 oz freshly grated
   Parmesan cheese, plus extra for
   sprinkling

salt and pepper

CHICKEN & MUSHROOM LASAGNE

Preheat the oven to 190°C/375°F/Gas Mark 5. To make the sauce, heat the oil in a large heavy-based saucepan. Add the garlic, onion and mushrooms and cook, stirring frequently, for 6 minutes. Add the chicken mince, chicken livers and Parma ham and cook over a low heat for 12 minutes, or until the meat has browned.

Stir the Marsala, tomatoes, basil and tomato purée into the mixture and cook for 4 minutes. Season to taste with salt and pepper, cover and leave to simmer for 30 minutes. Uncover, stir and simmer for a further 15 minutes.

Arrange sheets of lasagne over the base of an ovenproof dish, spoon over a layer of the mushroom sauce, then spoon over a layer of Béchamel Sauce. Place another layer of lasagne on top and repeat the process twice, finishing with a layer of Béchamel Sauce. Sprinkle over the grated Parmesan cheese and bake in the preheated oven for 35 minutes, or until golden brown and bubbling. Serve immediately.

SERVES 4

14 dried no pre-cook lasagne sheets

850 ml/1½ pints Béchamel Sauce (see page 7)

85 g/3 oz grated Parmesan cheese

wild mushroom sauce

2 tbsp olive oil

2 garlic cloves, crushed

1 large onion, finely chopped

225 g/8 oz wild mushrooms, sliced

300 g/10½ oz fresh chicken mince

85 g/3 oz chicken livers, finely chopped

115 g/4 oz Parma ham, diced

150 ml/5 fl oz Marsala

280 g/10 oz canned chopped tomatoes

1 tbsp chopped fresh basil leaves

2 tbsp tomato purée

salt and pepper

LASAGNE ALLA MARINARA

Preheat the oven to 190°C/375°F/Gas Mark 5. Melt the butter in a large heavy-based saucepan. Add the prawns and monkfish and cook over a medium heat for 3–5 minutes, or until the prawns change colour. Transfer the prawns to a small heatproof bowl with a slotted spoon. Add the mushrooms to the saucepan and cook, stirring occasionally, for 5 minutes. Transfer the fish and mushrooms to the bowl.

Stir the fish mixture, with any juices, into the Béchamel Sauce and season to taste with salt and pepper. Layer the tomatoes, chervil, basil, Béchamel Sauce mixture and lasagne sheets in a large ovenproof dish, ending with a layer of the fish mixture. Sprinkle evenly with the grated Parmesan cheese.

Bake in the preheated oven for 35 minutes, or until golden brown, then serve immediately.

SERVES 6

15 g/½ oz butter

225 g/8 oz raw prawns, peeled and deveined

450 g/1 lb monkfish fillets, skinned and chopped

225 g/8 oz chestnut mushrooms, chopped

850 ml/1½ pints Béchamel Sauce (see page 7)

400 g/14 oz canned chopped tomatoes

1 tbsp chopped fresh chervil

1 tbsp shredded fresh basil

175 g/6 oz dried no pre-cook lasagne sheets

85 g/3 oz freshly grated Parmesan cheese

salt and pepper

VEGETABLE LASAGNE

Preheat the oven to 200°C/400°F/Gas Mark 6. Brush a large ovenproof dish with oil. Brush a large griddle pan with oil and heat until smoking. Add half the aubergines and cook over a medium heat for 8 minutes, or until golden brown all over. Remove from the griddle pan and drain on kitchen paper. Add the remaining aubergine slices and extra oil, if necessary, and cook for 8 minutes, or until golden brown all over.

Melt the butter in a frying pan and add the garlic, courgettes, parsley and marjoram. Cook over a medium heat, stirring frequently, for 5 minutes, or until the courgettes are golden brown all over. Remove from the frying pan and leave to drain on kitchen paper.

Layer the aubergines, courgettes, mozzarella, passata and lasagne sheets in the dish, seasoning to taste with salt and pepper as you go and finishing with a layer of lasagne. Pour over the Béchamel Sauce, making sure that all the pasta is covered. Sprinkle with the grated Parmesan cheese and bake in the preheated oven for 30–40 minutes, or until golden brown. Serve immediately.

SERVES 4

olive oil, for brushing

2 aubergines, sliced

25 g/1 oz butter

1 garlic clove, finely chopped

4 courgettes, sliced

1 tbsp finely chopped fresh flat-leaf parsley

1 tbsp finely chopped fresh marjoram

225 g/8 oz mozzarella cheese, grated

600 ml/1 pint passata

175 g/6 oz dried no pre-cook lasagne sheets

600 ml/1 pint Béchamel Sauce (see page 7)

55 g/2 oz freshly grated Parmesan cheese

salt and pepper

CANNELLONI WITH HAM & RICOTTA

Preheat the oven to 180°C/350°F/Gas Mark 4. Heat the oil in a large heavy-based frying pan. Add the onions and garlic and cook over a low heat, stirring occasionally, for 5 minutes, or until the onion is softened. Add the basil, tomatoes and their can juices and tomato purée and season to taste with salt and pepper. Reduce the heat and simmer for 30 minutes, or until thickened.

Meanwhile, bring a large heavy-based saucepan of lightly salted water to the boil. Add the cannelloni tubes, return to the boil and cook for 8–10 minutes, or until tender but still firm to the bite. Using a slotted spoon, transfer the cannelloni tubes to a large plate and pat dry with kitchen paper.

Grease a large, shallow ovenproof dish with butter. Mix the ricotta, ham and egg together in a bowl and season to taste with salt and pepper. Using a teaspoon, fill the cannelloni tubes with the ricotta mixture and place in a single layer in the dish. Pour the tomato sauce over the cannelloni and sprinkle with the grated pecorino cheese. Bake in the preheated oven for 30 minutes, or until golden brown. Serve immediately.

SERVES 4

2 tbsp olive oil

2 onions, chopped

2 garlic cloves, finely chopped

1 tbsp shredded fresh basil

800 g/1 lb 12 oz canned chopped tomatoes

1 tbsp tomato purée

10–12 dried cannelloni tubes

butter, for greasing

225 g/8 oz ricotta cheese

115 g/4 oz cooked ham, diced

1 egg

55 g/2 oz freshly grated pecorino cheese

salt and pepper

VEGETABLE CANNELLONI

Preheat the oven to 190°C/375°F/Gas Mark 5. Bring a large heavy-bottom saucepan of lightly salted water to the boil. Add the cannelloni tubes, return to the boil and cook for 8–10 minutes, or until tender but still firm to the bite. Transfer the pasta to a plate and pat dry with kitchen paper. Brush a large ovenproof dish with oil.

Cut the aubergine into small dice. Heat the oil in a frying pan over a medium heat. Add the aubergine and cook, stirring frequently, for about 2–3 minutes.

Add the spinach, garlic, cumin and mushrooms and reduce the heat. Season to taste with salt and pepper and cook, stirring, for about 2–3 minutes. Spoon the mixture into the cannelloni tubes and put into the dish in a single layer.

To make the sauce, heat the oil in a pan over a medium heat. Add the onion and garlic and cook for 1 minute. Add the tomatoes, sugar and basil and bring to the boil. Reduce the heat and simmer for about 5 minutes. Spoon the sauce over the cannelloni tubes.

Arrange the mozzarella cheese on top of the sauce and bake in the preheated oven for about 30 minutes, or until the cheese is golden brown and bubbling. Serve garnished with lamb's lettuce.

SERVES 4

12 dried cannelloni tubes

1 aubergine

125 ml/4 fl oz olive oil, plus extra for brushing

225 g/8 oz spinach

2 garlic cloves, crushed

1 tsp ground cumin

85 g/3 oz mushrooms, chopped

55 g/2 oz mozzarella cheese, sliced

salt and pepper

lamb's lettuce, to garnish

tomato sauce

1 tbsp olive oil

1 onion, chopped

2 garlic cloves, crushed

800 g/1 lb 12 oz canned chopped tomatoes

1 tsp caster sugar

2 tbsp chopped fresh basil

HOT TOMATO & CONCHIGLIE GRATIN

Put the onion, tomatoes and milk in a large heavy-based saucepan and bring just to the boil. Add the chillies, garlic, coriander and pasta, season to taste with salt and pepper and cook over a medium heat, stirring frequently, for 2–3 minutes.

Add just enough water to cover and cook, stirring frequently, for 8–10 minutes, until the pasta is tender but still firm to the bite. Meanwhile, preheat the grill.

Spoon the pasta mixture into individual flameproof dishes and sprinkle evenly with the cheese. Place under the grill for 3–4 minutes, until the cheese has melted. Serve immediately.

SERVES 4

1 onion, chopped

400 g/14 oz canned chopped tomatoes

225 ml/8 fl oz milk

1–2 red chillies, deseeded and finely chopped

1 garlic clove, finely chopped

pinch of ground coriander

280 g/10 oz dried conchiglie

85 g/3 oz Gruyère cheese, grated

salt and pepper

BEEF & MACARONI SOUFFLÉ

Preheat the oven to 190°C/375°F/Gas Mark 5. Heat the oil in a large heavy-based frying pan. Add the onion and cook over a low heat, stirring occasionally, for 5 minutes, or until softened. Add the beef and cook, breaking up the meat with a wooden spoon, until browned. Stir in the garlic, tomatoes and their can juices and tomato purée, then season to taste with salt and pepper. Bring to the boil, reduce the heat and simmer for 20 minutes, then remove the frying pan from the heat and leave to cool slightly.

Meanwhile, bring a large heavy-based saucepan of lightly salted water to the boil. Add the pasta, return to the boil and cook for 8–10 minutes, or until tender but still firm to the bite. Drain and reserve.

Lightly grease a 1.5-litre/2¾-pint soufflé dish with butter. Beat the egg yolks and add them to the meat sauce, then stir in the pasta. Whisk the egg whites until stiff peaks form, then fold into the sauce. Spoon the mixture into the dish, sprinkle with the grated Parmesan cheese and bake in the preheated oven for 45 minutes, or until well risen and golden brown. Sprinkle with extra grated Parmesan cheese and serve immediately.

SERVES 4

2 tbsp olive oil

1 large onion, chopped

225 g/8 oz fresh beef mince

1 garlic clove, finely chopped

400 g/14 oz canned chopped tomatoes

1 tbsp tomato purée

175 g/6 oz dried macaroni

butter, for greasing

3 eggs, separated

40 g/1½ oz freshly grated Parmesan cheese, plus extra to serve

salt and pepper

PASTICCIO

Preheat the oven to 190°C/375°F/Gas Mark 5. Heat the oil in a large heavy-based frying pan. Add the onion and garlic and cook over a low heat, stirring occasionally, for 5 minutes, or until softened. Add the lamb and cook, breaking it up with a wooden spoon, until browned all over. Add the tomato purée and sprinkle in the flour. Cook, stirring, for 1 minute, then stir in the stock. Season to taste with salt and pepper and stir in the cinnamon. Bring to the boil, reduce the heat, cover and cook for 25 minutes.

Meanwhile, bring a large heavy-based saucepan of lightly salted water to the boil. Add the pasta, return to the boil and cook for 8–10 minutes, or until tender but still firm to the bite.

Drain the pasta and stir into the lamb mixture. Spoon into a large ovenproof dish and arrange the tomato slices on top. Beat together the yogurt and eggs then spoon over the lamb evenly. Bake in the preheated oven for 1 hour. Serve immediately.

SERVES 4

1 tbsp olive oil

1 onion, chopped

2 garlic cloves, finely chopped

450 g/1 lb fresh lamb mince

2 tbsp tomato purée

2 tbsp plain flour

300 ml/10 fl oz chicken stock

1 tsp ground cinnamon

115 g/4 oz dried macaroni

2 beef tomatoes, sliced

300 ml/10 fl oz Greek yogurt

2 eggs, lightly beaten

salt and pepper

BAKED TUNA & RICOTTA RIGATONI

Preheat the oven to 200°C/400°F/Gas Mark 6. Lightly grease a large ovenproof dish with butter. Bring a large heavy-based saucepan of lightly salted water to the boil. Add the rigatoni, return to the boil and cook for 8–10 minutes, or until just tender but still firm to the bite. Drain the pasta and leave until cool enough to handle.

Meanwhile, mix the tuna and ricotta cheese together in a bowl to form a soft paste. Spoon the mixture into a piping bag and use to fill the rigatoni. Arrange the filled pasta tubes side by side in the prepared dish.

To make the sauce, mix the cream and Parmesan cheese together in a bowl and season to taste with salt and pepper. Spoon the sauce over the rigatoni and top with the sun-dried tomatoes, arranged in a criss-cross pattern. Bake in the preheated oven for 20 minutes. Serve hot straight from the dish.

SERVES 4

butter, for greasing

450 g/1 lb dried rigatoni

200 g/7 oz canned flaked tuna, drained

225 g/8 oz ricotta cheese

125 ml/4 fl oz double cream

225 g/8 oz freshly grated Parmesan cheese

115 g/4 oz sun-dried tomatoes, drained and sliced

salt and pepper

MACARONI & SEAFOOD BAKE

Preheat the oven to 180°C/350°F/Gas Mark 4. Bring a large saucepan of lightly salted water to the boil. Add the pasta, return to the boil and cook for 8–10 minutes, or until tender but still firm to the bite. Drain and return to the saucepan. Add 25 g/1 oz of the butter to the pasta, cover, shake the saucepan and keep warm.

Melt the remaining butter in a separate saucepan. Add the fennel and cook for 3–4 minutes. Stir in the mushrooms and cook for a further 2 minutes. Stir in the prawns, then remove the saucepan from the heat.

Stir the cooked pasta, cayenne pepper and prawn mixture into the Béchamel Sauce.

Grease a large ovenproof dish, then pour the mixture into the dish and spread evenly. Sprinkle over the Parmesan cheese and arrange the tomato slices in a ring around the edge. Brush the tomatoes with oil, then sprinkle over the oregano. Bake in the preheated oven for 25 minutes, or until golden brown. Serve immediately.

SERVES 4

350 g/12 oz dried macaroni

85 g/3 oz butter, plus extra for greasing

2 small fennel bulbs, trimmed and thinly sliced

175 g/6 oz mushrooms, thinly sliced

175 g/6 oz cooked peeled prawns

pinch of cayenne pepper

600 ml/1 pint Béchamel Sauce (see page 7)

55 g/2 oz freshly grated Parmesan cheese

2 large tomatoes, halved and sliced

olive oil, for brushing

1 tsp dried oregano

salt

MACARONI CHEESE & TOMATO

Preheat the oven to 190ºC/375ºF/Gas Mark 5. Grease a deep ovenproof dish with a little butter.

To make the tomato sauce, heat the oil in a pan over a medium heat. Add the shallot and garlic and cook, stirring constantly, for 1 minute. Add the tomatoes and basil and season to taste with salt and pepper. Cook, stirring, for 10 minutes.

Meanwhile, bring a large pan of lightly salted water to the boil over a medium heat. Add the macaroni and cook for 8–10 minutes, or until tender but still firm to the bite. Drain well.

Mix the grated Cheddar and Parmesan cheeses together in a small bowl. Spoon one third of the tomato sauce into the base of the prepared dish, then cover with one third of the macaroni and top with one third of the mixed cheeses. Season to taste with salt and pepper. Repeat these layers twice, ending with a layer of the grated cheeses.

Mix the breadcrumbs and basil together and sprinkle evenly over the top. Dot the topping with the butter and cook in the preheated oven for about 25 minutes, or until the topping is golden brown and bubbling. Serve.

SERVES 4

225 g/8 oz dried macaroni

175 g/6 oz freshly grated Cheddar cheese

100 g/3½ oz freshly grated Parmesan cheese

4 tbsp fresh white breadcrumbs

1 tbsp chopped fresh basil

1 tbsp butter or margarine, plus extra for greasing

salt and pepper

tomato sauce

1 tbsp olive oil

1 shallot, finely chopped

2 garlic cloves, crushed

500 g/1 lb 2 oz canned chopped tomatoes

1 tbsp chopped fresh basil

salt and pepper

MIXED
VEGETABLE
AGNOLOTTI

To make the filling, heat the oil in a large heavy-based saucepan. Add the onion and garlic and cook over a low heat, stirring occasionally, for 5 minutes, or until softened. Add the aubergines, courgettes, tomatoes, green and red peppers, sun-dried tomato paste and basil. Season to taste with salt and pepper, cover and simmer gently, stirring occasionally, for 20 minutes.

Lightly grease an ovenproof dish with butter. Roll out the pasta dough on a lightly floured work surface and stamp out 7.5-cm/ 3-inch rounds with a fluted biscuit cutter. Place a spoonful of the vegetable filling on each round. Dampen the edges slightly and fold the pasta rounds over, pressing together to seal. Place on a floured tea towel and leave to stand for 1 hour. Preheat the oven to 200°C/400°F/Gas Mark 6.

Bring a large saucepan of lightly salted water to the boil. Add the agnolotti, in batches if necessary, return to the boil and cook for 3–4 minutes. Remove with a slotted spoon, drain and transfer to the prepared dish. Sprinkle with the Parmesan cheese and bake in the preheated oven for 20 minutes. Serve immediately.

SERVES 4

butter, for greasing

1 quantity Basic Pasta Dough (see page 8)

plain flour, for dusting

85 g/3 oz freshly grated Parmesan

salt

filling

125 ml/4 fl oz olive oil

1 red onion, chopped

3 garlic cloves, chopped

2 large aubergines, cut into chunks

3 large courgettes, cut into chunks

6 beef tomatoes, peeled, deseeded and roughly chopped

1 large green pepper, deseeded and diced

1 large red pepper, deseeded and diced

1 tbsp sun-dried tomato paste

1 tbsp shredded fresh basil

salt and pepper

GARLIC MUSHROOM RAVIOLI

Heat 25 g/1 oz of the butter in a frying pan. Add the shallots, 1 crushed garlic clove, the mushrooms and celery and cook for 4–5 minutes. Remove the frying pan from the heat, stir in the pecorino cheese and season to taste with salt and pepper.

Divide the pasta dough in half and wrap 1 piece in clingfilm. Roll out the other piece on a lightly floured surface to a rectangle 2–3 mm/$\frac{1}{16}$–$\frac{1}{8}$ inch thick. Cover with a damp tea towel and roll out the other piece of dough to the same size. Place small mounds, about 1 teaspoon each, of the filling in rows 4 cm/1½ inches apart on a sheet of pasta dough. Brush the spaces between the mounds with the beaten egg. Lift the second sheet of dough on top of the first and press down firmly between the pockets of filling, pushing out any air bubbles. Using a pasta wheel or sharp knife, cut into squares. Place on a floured tea towel and leave to stand for 1 hour.

Bring a large heavy-based saucepan of water to the boil, add the ravioli and cook in batches for 2–3 minutes, or until cooked. Remove with a slotted spoon and drain thoroughly.

Meanwhile, melt the remaining butter in a frying pan. Add the remaining garlic and plenty of pepper and cook for 1–2 minutes. Transfer the ravioli to serving plates and pour over the garlic butter. Garnish with grated pecorino cheese and serve immediately.

SERVES 4

75 g/2¾ oz butter

50 g/1¾ oz shallots, finely chopped

3 garlic cloves, crushed

50 g/1¾ oz mushrooms, wiped and finely chopped

½ celery stick, finely chopped

25 g/1 oz pecorino cheese, finely grated, plus extra to serve

½ quantity Basic Pasta Dough (see page 8)

plain flour, for dusting

1 egg, lightly beaten

salt and pepper

CREAMY CHICKEN RAVIOLI

Place the chicken, spinach, prosciutto and shallot in a food processor and process until chopped and blended. Transfer to a bowl, stir in 2 tablespoons of the pecorino cheese, the nutmeg and 1 of the eggs. Season to taste with salt and pepper.

Divide the pasta dough in half and wrap 1 piece in clingfilm. Roll out the other piece on a lightly floured surface to a rectangle 2–3 mm/$\frac{1}{16}$–$\frac{1}{8}$ inch thick. Cover with a damp tea towel and roll out the other piece of dough to the same size. Place small mounds, about 1 teaspoon each, of the filling in rows 4 cm/1½ inches apart on a sheet of pasta dough. Brush the spaces between the mounds with the remaining beaten egg. Lift the second sheet of dough on top of the first and press down firmly between the pockets of filling, pushing out any air bubbles. Using a pasta wheel or sharp knife, cut into squares. Place on a floured tea towel and leave to stand for 1 hour.

Bring a large saucepan of lightly salted water to the boil. Add the ravioli in batches and cook for 5 minutes. Remove with a slotted spoon, drain and transfer to a warmed dish.

Meanwhile, pour the cream into a frying pan, add the garlic and bring to the boil. Simmer for 1 minute, then add the mushrooms and 2 tablespoons of the remaining cheese. Season and simmer for 3 minutes. Stir in the basil, then pour the sauce over the ravioli. Sprinkle with the remaining cheese, garnish with basil and serve.

SERVES 4

115 g/4 oz cooked skinless, boneless chicken breast, roughly chopped

55 g/2 oz cooked spinach

55 g/2 oz prosciutto, roughly chopped

1 shallot, roughly chopped

6 tbsp freshly grated pecorino cheese

pinch of freshly grated nutmeg

2 eggs, lightly beaten

1 quantity Basic Pasta Dough (see page 8)

plain flour, for dusting

300 ml/10 fl oz double cream

2 garlic cloves, finely chopped

115 g/4 oz chestnut mushrooms, thinly sliced

2 tbsp shredded fresh basil, plus extra sprigs to garnish

salt and pepper

BEEF RAVIOLI

Heat the oil and half the butter in a large saucepan. Add the beef and cook over a medium heat for 8–10 minutes. Remove the beef from the pan. Reduce the heat and add the onion, celery and carrot to the pan. Cook for 5 minutes, until softened. Return the beef to the pan, add the wine and cook until reduced by two thirds. Combine the stock and tomato purée, stir into the pan and season. Cover and simmer very gently for 3 hours, until the meat is tender and the sauce has thickened. Remove the beef from the pan and leave to cool slightly.

Mix the breadcrumbs and half the Parmesan and stir in about half the sauce (discard the remaining sauce). Finely chop the beef and stir it into the breadcrumb mixture. Season and stir in the nutmeg, cinnamon and eggs.

Roll out the pasta dough on a lightly floured surface to 2–3 mm/ $\frac{1}{16}$–$\frac{1}{8}$ inch thick. Using a fluted 5-cm/2-inch biscuit cutter, stamp out rounds. Place about 1 teaspoon of the beef mixture in the centre of each round, brush the edges with water, and fold in half, pressing the edges to seal. Place on a floured tea towel and leave to stand for 30 minutes.

Bring a pan of salted water to the boil. Add the ravioli and cook for 5–8 minutes, until tender. Meanwhile, melt the remaining butter. Drain the ravioli and place in a serving dish. Pour over the melted butter, sprinkle with the remaining Parmesan and serve.

SERVES 6

3 tbsp olive oil

70 g/2½ oz butter

350 g/12 oz stewing beef, in a single piece

1 red onion, finely chopped

1 celery stick, finely chopped

1 carrot, finely chopped

150 ml/5 fl oz red wine

225 ml/8 fl oz beef stock

1 tbsp tomato purée

55 g/2 oz fresh breadcrumbs

4 tbsp freshly grated Parmesan cheese

pinch of freshly grated nutmeg

pinch of ground cinnamon

2 eggs, lightly beaten

1½ quantities Basic Pasta Dough (see page 8)

plain flour, for dusting

salt and pepper

CRAB RAVIOLI

Thinly slice the spring onions, keeping the white and green parts separate. Mix the green spring onions, crabmeat, ginger and chilli sauce to taste together in a bowl. Cover and chill.

Place the tomatoes in a food processor and process to a purée. Place the garlic, white spring onions and vinegar in a saucepan and add the puréed tomatoes. Bring to the boil, then reduce the heat and simmer for 10 minutes. Remove from the heat and reserve.

Divide the pasta dough in half and wrap 1 piece in clingfilm. Roll out the other piece on a lightly floured surface to a rectangle 2–3 mm/$\frac{1}{16}$–$\frac{1}{8}$ inch thick. Cover with a damp tea towel and roll out the other piece of dough to the same size. Place small mounds, about 1 teaspoon each, of the filling in rows 4 cm/1½ inches apart on a sheet of pasta dough. Brush the spaces between the mounds with beaten egg. Lift the second sheet of dough on top of the first and press down firmly between the pockets of filling, pushing out any air bubbles. Using a pasta wheel or sharp knife, cut into squares. Place on a floured tea towel and leave to stand for 1 hour.

Bring a large saucepan of lightly salted water to the boil. Add the ravioli and cook for 5 minutes. Remove with a slotted spoon and drain on kitchen paper. Gently heat the tomato sauce and whisk in the cream. Place the ravioli on serving plates, pour over the sauce, garnish with shredded spring onion and serve.

SERVES 4

6 spring onions

350 g/12 oz crabmeat

2 tsp finely chopped fresh ginger

$\frac{1}{8}$–$\frac{1}{4}$ tsp chilli sauce or Tabasco sauce

700 g/1 lb 9 oz tomatoes, peeled, deseeded and roughly chopped

1 garlic clove, finely chopped

1 tbsp white wine vinegar

1 quantity Basic Pasta Dough (see page 8)

plain flour, for dusting

1 egg, lightly beaten

2 tbsp double cream

salt

shredded spring onion, to garnish

INDEX